Ioanna Dimakou

THE
path
FROM
fear
TO
fearless
ness

MEGAS SEIRIOS
Publications

ISBN: 978-960-7350-36-7

This book is published by **Megas Seirios Publications**, founded by the **Servers' Society Spiritual Centre** based in Athens, Greece. To find more information about the mission, works and activities of the Society and/or to place an order, please visit our website:
www.megas-seirios.gr

or contact us at:
9, Sarantaporou Street, Athens, Greece, P.O.: 111 44
e-mail: info@megas-seirios.gr
Tel.: +30 210 20 15 194
Fax: +30 210 22 30 864

Translation from Greek: Geoffrey Cox

Cover and book design: Marianna Smyrniotou

I dedicate this book
to Mrs Klairi Lykiardopoulou,
who by her constant
and unswerving support
has helped me and always helps me
in my difficult progress
from fear to fearlessness.

☙

CONTENTS

INTRODUCTION

Some five months had passed since the day of my first meeting with the Master, the founder of the Servers' Society spiritual centre, when, at one of our meetings, he interrupted me as I was reading out of my diary and asked me:

"Mrs Ioanna, have you realised that you are already writing a book?"

Since I didn't fully understand the question and accustomed as I was to his not interrupting me when I read my monotonous diary by the hour, I went on reading.

But, shortly, without having heard a word of what I had managed to read, he pursued his line of thought by saying:

"The moment you realise that by working on this book you will help some of your fellow-beings to overcome problems the same as your own, from the moment that your heart fills with real love, the minor troubles which you continue to have will automatically stop. I think that the time has come for you to write this book. I think the time has come for you to become a spiritual person."

How little, in fact, did I understand at that moment the real significance of his words! But what I knew very well was that I was not going to escape easily. I knew that when the Master said something, he meant it, and so I sat there looking at him, thunderstruck, without the strength even to refuse.

His voice brought me back to reality when he said to me:

"So what do you say? Will you try to write the book – since, in any case, it's almost written in your diary?"

"How can you ask me, Master, to do something like that? What connection can I possibly have with authorship? I was never any good at writing. And you know that my studies had nothing to do with all that. I would very much like to write not one but many books – and works of literature at that – but, as you must realise, it's impossible in the nature of things."

After my negative reply, and in such a categorical way, I was convinced that he would change his mind. But to my surprise, I heard him say:

"I am sure that you are in a position to write this book and I want you to think again. We will conclude our conversation this evening by saying that. Isn't it selfish on your part for you to know that many of your fellow human beings have the same problems as you and that you can help some of them by handing on to them what you have learnt, but not to wish even to try?"

It was these words, and obtaining the valuable help of Mrs Klairi Lykiardopoulou, without whose guidance I would certainly not have managed to do anything, which played a decisive role in my taking the decision on the writing of this book.

Because I realised that the Master was not asking me to write any literary work, but simply to describe the way in which my therapy had gone forward through my discipleship, and how I learnt to overcome my problems. He was asking me, that is, to explain how I learnt to cope with life. Because life means problems, and when you don't know how to overcome them in the right way, they lead you to despair and illness.

It was these words of the Master which gave me strength to begin writing again every time that I had stopped for long periods, determined not to continue. They made me believe that a book written by me, after only a few months discipleship with the Master, would be useful and could help some of my fellow human beings.

At this point I have to say that I too had felt the need for such a book, on a completely different level from that in which Mrs Klairi Lykiardopoulou has set down the teaching which I was receiving, long before the Master made his proposal. Moreover, at that time I had asked Mrs Klairi to write it. But she was writing something else at the time and it wasn't possible for her to do it. "Perhaps", she told me, "this will happen later".

There are two reasons why I felt this need at a very early stage. The first is the fact that in order to attend lessons at the Society, where you have the opportunity to receive the teaching on the basis of a programme and depending upon your abilities, a condition is that you should have free time and live in Athens. Of course, you can also receive the lessons by correspondence. But in cases like mine, this would have produced no results.

The second was that although Mrs Klairi has covered the teaching by means of her books, these are addressed to people who can, first of all, concentrate on reading them and go deeply into their meanings. But people with mental illnesses such as myself need books written at a simple level, and with examples which relate to our situation, through which we can find the solution to our problems.

"The roads", the Master says, "which lead man to reach the point where he can on his own find the right solutions and have the right positions and views on life are many, but they all start out from a common point: love."

In the chapters which follow, I shall attempt to give an account of all the teachings I received from the Master which concern my progress – still continuing today – in discovering and expressing my own reserves of love.

HOW I GOT TO KNOW
THE SOCIETY

It was some years now since my son Dionysis, who is now 30 years old, told me that he had begun to attend lessons in self-knowledge at the Servers' Society spiritual centre. I asked him at that time if I could visit the Society, not because I wanted to attend lessons as well, since I believed that I knew everything – and, naturally, myself – but because I wanted to find out what, roughly, this spiritual centre teaches its members. And so it came about that my son arranged a meeting with the President of the Society and writer Mrs Klairi Lykiardopoulou.

Before I met Mrs Klairi in her office, I had the opportunity to get to know the Society's premises as my son took me on a guided tour, and I had to admit that this was a pleasant and warm environment, and the many vases of freshly-cut flowers which had been placed at many points gave it a very cheerful note. During my tour, the following surprise awaited me. Although I had expected to find on the premises of the Society only individuals of a certain age, probably with difficulties and problems, I saw, on the contrary, plenty of young people of both genders with smiling faces which suggested people who knew what they want from life. When I then met Mrs Klairi, her personality impressed me; it emitted simultaneously strength and calm and showed that she was an integrated person.

The first thing which I asked of her was that she should tell me a little about the purpose for which the Society had been set up. She explained to me that it was founded as a result of the urge of certain people to respond to the great needs of society with the guidance of the philosopher and writer Dimitris Kakalidis, whom all the members call 'Master'. It has no financial, political, or religious support from anyone at all, and its only income is from the small subscription paid by the members to meet its expenses. Furthermore, she stressed that every form of service is performed without personal gain.

"And what is the content of the teaching at the Society?"

"Our teaching concerns study to gain knowledge of the truth, about life, the world, love, God. This study leads to the realisation that we are part of the miracle of God and that we have the power to make this miracle reality at any time, changing illness into health and sorrow into joy, making, that is, darkness light."

It is a fact that at that time I understood very little of the importance of these words, but what I did understand was that I was lucky that my son spent some of his free time in getting to know himself, and not in billiard halls and bars.

I had another meeting with Mrs Klairi three years later. This took place at the time when I had started to have symptoms of my illness. I suffered from various phobias which limited my life. Dionysis had asked her to see me and to talk to me, and she received me one evening.

From the conversation which we had she understood that my problems were psychological, and she tried to explain to me what they were due to. But I didn't retain a single world of what she said to me. I was in such a state of anxiety that it was impossible for me to concentrate on the conversation. I left the Society disillusioned, because at the time I still hadn't realised that no one could cure me if I hadn't first decided to work on improving myself.

Three years passed after my second contact with the Society. Three years of suffering for me. In that space of time I had visited many doctors.

17

At my side all these years were my husband, my daughter, and my son. Each of them supported me in their own way. My husband with great understanding and patience. My daughter at the time when I became ill was abroad working on her postgraduate degree. In the period when she was away, I was not able to be with her, even though she had asked me to go many times. My condition did not permit me to undertake so long a journey. Each time I gave her one excuse or another, because I was afraid that if she learnt the truth, she would interrupt her studies in order to be with me. On her return to us, after taking her degree, things got better for all of us. Now there was a housewife at home.

The one who supported me with the greatest patience was my son. He had spent countless hours in doctors' waiting-rooms, waiting for me to finish with some examination which I'd taken it into my head to have done. And he never resented that. Always, with a smile on his lips, he attempted to cheer me up. I didn't realise then that the way he dealt with problems and life had been taught to him at the Society.

One evening, after I had gone through a major panic crisis, I heard Dionysis say to me:

"What do you say, Mother? Shall I ask the Master to see you, so that you can ask for his help with your problem?"

I'd come to believe so strongly that no one could help me that my son's question gave me hope.

"Very well, Dionysis, ask him to make an appointment for us", I told him.

As soon as I had given my consent, a thousand thoughts started to flood into my mind, and the questions came one after the other:

"And what can the Master do for me?"

"So has it something to do with psychotherapy?"

"How shall I manage to get there, since I'm afraid to go out of the house, and for how long shall I have to see him?"

"Will he see me soon?"

"And if he tells me to stop taking the pills, what shall I do?"

In the state which I was in I saw everything in the blackest colours. And so I gave negative answers to my questions myself, and these were not slow in bringing me to a state of panic. My son tried to calm me down in vain. I wasn't able to think. In the end, as always, I resorted again to taking a tranquilliser.

That night I slept very little, and my sleep was very troubled. Every so often I woke up with acute tachycardia. It wasn't, of course, the first time that I had felt all these symptoms. Whenever I was to see some doctor or do some test, the days before were days of torment for me. The only thought that calmed me a little was that no one was forcing me to go to this meeting and that I had plenty of time in front of me to think again.

MY FIRST MEETING
WITH THE MASTER

On the day when it had been arranged that I should have my first meeting with the Master, my anxiety was at the top of the scale. One question constantly went round and round in my mind:

"Will the Master be able to help me over my problem? And if so, how?"

Dionysis and I arrived at the Society – after I had first taken a tranquilliser. When I climbed the stairs, I had tachycardia, I felt faint, and my legs shook so much that I thought I would collapse. I was ready to change my plans and leave, but the touch of Dionysis' hand brought me round, and I thought to myself:

"Ioanna, this is your last chance. You can't go on living like this, or, rather, you can't die every day of fear – and make all your loved ones suffer as well. You must seek the help of the Master. Perhaps he will be able to help you."

It was these thoughts which made me climb the rest of the stairs and enter the Society's sitting-room. Five minutes later, we went into the room where the Master was; apart from him, Mrs Klairi was also there. I collapsed – literally – on to a seat and began to look at the Master. I had before me a man younger than myself, with a serene face. The tone of his voice suggested someone with a strong will and with power.

A part of his calm communicated itself to me at once, and so, when in a little while I started to explain to him what my problems were, I shook a good deal less than before. I told him that everything had started three years before, completely out of the blue: when I was with some friends in the courtyard of our house, I felt faint, my heart began to race, and at the same time I felt acute discomfort in the abdomen. I thought that I must be suffering from some kind of food poisoning, and so I didn't worry. This situation continued until two in the morning.

The next day, I went down to the offices of our family business, which is the importation of spare parts, to which, after I had retired from the public service with a pension, I went in the mornings to help my husband.

After a short while, I set off from there to see to various jobs, which included a visit to a bank. I'd taken my place in the queue, waiting to make the transaction I wanted, when I suddenly felt the same dizziness, the same tachycardia as before, and I almost fell down in a faint. I left the bank, without completing my business, took a taxi, and returned to the office.

The next step was a visit to a doctor, and the various tests that he sent me to have done, which showed that I had nothing pathological. The doctor's diagnosis was that my symptoms were due to the menopause. A year later, I was in a much worse state. I had begun to be afraid to go out, I couldn't go into shops, or generally to places where there were people. I stopped my visits to friends' houses, and in the end I didn't want anyone to come to our house, because I was seized by a panic crisis.

At that time, as I was always shut up inside, I began to read books in connection with my case. Books by psychiatrists, gynaecologists, and I asked Dionysis to supply me with any other kind which I believed could help me. As a result of all this study, I reached the conclusion that my problem was not due to the menopause, but must be psychological.

I began to visit one psychiatrist after another. The diagnoses of all of them were that I was suffering from agoraphobia, from generalised anxiety, and a concealed form of depression. They started to give me various drugs, and, above all, tranquillisers. For a short time, and as long as the doses of the drugs were high, the symptoms became milder. Later, however, I went back to the state I had been in before.

Three years later, I had arrived at the point of spending most of my time curled up on the sofa of our sitting-room, shaking. But the most tragic thing was that I was unable to sit at the table and eat with my husband and children, because I was seized with agitation. I had begun, that is, to have a problem even with the members of my family. I then told the Master that before these symptoms had presented themselves, and within a ten-year period, I had lost four loved ones from my family, whose loss cost me dearly.

While I was talking, the Master didn't interrupt me at all. He listened to me with patience and waited for me to finish. He then told me the following:

"Your problem is not just a present one, and is due to the fact that you deal with some things in life in a wrong way. You have learnt for the solution of your problems, but also in your relations with other people, to use only your emotions. But problems must be dealt with by the mind, the reason, and love. The same with people. The emotions follow. If this doesn't happen, the emotions make us sick. We must solve problems with reason, and, relying on that, become masters of situations, learning in this way to distinguish our thoughts from our emotions. But always we shall use love."

At this point I asked the Master:

"Since, as you say, my problem is not of the present and is due to a wrong approach to my problems, why is it that all these symptoms have presented themselves now, and not earlier?"

"Because women, up to the menopause and through sexual relations, diffuse their energies and the powers of the soul which they have inside them. After the menopause, however, a woman believes that life is finished for her, so that all the energies accumulate within her and make problems for her. She doesn't know that this is the period when she can open her embrace and take into it everybody and everything with love and with the mind, and can accept good things and bad things as the will of God."

"And now that I have told you what are the causes of your difficulties, and until you understand what I have explained to you and turn it into action, and since your most basic problem is your fear of going about outside on your own, you will do the following exercise: you will close your eyes and go down the stairs in your mind. You will go out, still in your mind, you will look at everything with love, and you'll come back again."

And so I closed my eyes and imagined myself going down the stairs, going outside, walking on the pavement, looking at everything with love, and then coming back again.

When I opened my eyes, the Master asked me:

"Have you done the exercise?"

"I have."

"And how did you feel?"

"I felt alarm and fear."

"Now you'll repeat it."

I repeated the exercise, and when I'd finished, he asked me:

"So – how did you feel this time?"

"Definitely better."

"And now what you've done in your mind, you're going to do in reality. You will get up, you will go down the stairs, you'll go outside, you will walk as far as the corner of the block, and you'll come back. But whatever you meet on the way you will embrace with love."

I got up from my seat trembling, and with my eyes sought the help of Dionysis, who was sitting next to me. But he didn't move from where he was sitting and I understood from his expression that he wasn't going to help me in the way I wanted. And so, having no choice, I opened the door and began, very gingerly, to go down the stairs leading to the ground floor. I felt my legs trembling so much that I had to get hold of the handrail so as not to fall. For a moment I thought of going back. The thought that I would be going out alone, among the crowd, chilled me. But I managed to put my mind to work and say to myself: "Ioanna, you have to try, it's your last chance."

In the event, I continued to go down the stairs, and, when I reached the ground floor, I opened the door and went out on to the little balcony which is in front of the entrance to the Society. There I stopped, because everything had started to swirl around me. I saw people walking in the street, the cars driving past, and I wondered: "How can I possibly go about among them? No, I can't do it. That's enough. I have to go back." But my thinking changed before I was able to put my decision into action, and I said: "You know that if you go back, there's no other opportunity of escaping from the hopeless situation you are in. So it's now or never!"

That was it! My feet came unstuck from the ground and I began to descend the few steps which lead to the pavement of the avenue. When I reached it, I began to walk cautiously. Soon my legs were shaking less, I felt less dizzy, as well as my anxiety being less, and in a little while I arrived at the corner of the block, and at that moment I shouted in happiness "I've done it!"

The return was easier. I walked more quickly, more steadily, and my gaze took in people with less fear. When I returned to the room from which I had set out, I believed that the first step in my cure had been taken. The Master welcomed me with a smile, and told me:

"Up to this point, you've done very well. I don't want to give you any other exercises today, or to analyse other matters, because I realise you must be tired. But before you leave, I'd like to recommend two things to you. The first is that you should begin again, little by little, to do your housework and cook for your family. But you must do both the jobs and the cooking with your mind and with love, and not mechanically. Before you start on any job, you will reflect that you are doing it to please your husband, your children, or your friends. In this way, everything will become easier and you won't be possessed by anxiety."

"The second thing I have to recommend is for you to think whether you really want to be made well – or whether you belong to that category of people who, although they could be well, don't want to be."

"And what am I to do about the drugs?"

"Consult your doctor about those. That's his job."

As I held out my hand to say good night to him and to thank him, he asked me:

"What did we say you will do if you feel any of your symptoms?"

"I will try to accept them and to deal with them with my mind, and I won't allow emotions to lead me astray so that my anxiety increases."

THE DECISION
FOR DISCIPLESHIP

Dawn on the day after my meeting with the Master found me sitting in bed with my eyes swollen with sleeplessness. All night I had been trying to put my thoughts in some kind of order. I called to mind again and again the conversation I had had with him, his analyses of the causes behind my problems, and, of course, the exercises he had set me to do.

One moment I would say to myself that he wouldn't be able to help me with words and exercises, since so many drugs that I'd taken hadn't succeeded in doing anything. So there was no need for me to go back to the Society. The next moment I said to myself that I couldn't reject his method of treatment when it hadn't even properly started yet.

There was a struggle going on inside me. I tried desperately to find some scientific basis to validate something of all that he'd said to me and to use it as a lifebelt.

I suddenly remembered that Isaac Marks, a professor of psychiatry, in his book 'Triumph over Phobia', refers to the exercise which the Master had given me as a method of psychotherapy. He says, among other things, that included among the methods of psychotherapy are flooding techniques. In these techniques, exposure to the phobia-creating situation can be in the mind, by means of slides and films, or by living exposure. The sooner you face up to the phobic object, the sooner there will be an improvement. And he concludes with the following saying:

> *"He wasn't able to try for fear he died.*
> *He never tried, and so he died."*

> *"He wasn't able to try for fear he died.*
> *When he tried, his fears died."*

Then what I had been told by the Professor of Clinical Psychology at the University of Crete, Ioannis Nestoros, who was the last doctor to treat me and whom I had visited for the first time a few days before my meeting with the Master, came to my mind.

When he had defined my problem exactly, he told me that he had come to the conclusion that all mental illnesses can be cured if the patient and his environment – and his doctor – believe that he can get well and he makes up his mind to work towards overcoming his problems, in accordance with the instructions of a specialist, of course.

About me, he said that he was sure that I could be cured – if I decided to face up to the situations which generated phobia. He told me in so many words: "The golden rule in these cases is the avoidance of flight. The essence of facing up to fear is that we should learn to guide it until the storm has passed. And an important role in this guidance is played by the individual's thoughts, which are responsible for the emotional charge which leads him into a state of anxiety. Man is capable of changing these thoughts."

He also told me that it would help me a great deal to follow a programme of elimination of my phobias and to set it in motion, without deviations, and that it would be a good idea for me to carry it out, to begin with at least, with some relative or friend to support me.

"And you see", I thought, "how the Master, on the very first day, in order to help me, used two of the three types of flooding techniques for the therapy of phobias. To begin with, he made me live my fears in my mind, and then deal with them in reality by living exposure to them –

and I managed it quite well. In addition, I mustn't forget the certainty with which he assured me that my cure depends chiefly on how far I am prepared to work, to change my way of thinking and of dealing with my problems, precisely as Mr Nestoros had told me. I think that I must put my trust in him." It was after all these thoughts that my first hope of being cured came to me.

The second issue which concerned me was the answer to the Master's question as to whether I really wanted to get well, or whether I belonged to that category of persons who, while they could be cured, don't wish to be. I excluded myself immediately from this second category and came to the conclusion that my greatest wish was to be able to overcome my problems as rapidly as possible, because I had given up all my activities and lived only with these problems. When I closed my eyes, exhausted, I had taken the decision that I would without fail try to put into practice what the Master would teach me in the future.

The next day, while I was eating my breakfast, I felt the familiar tightening of my heart and a faint dizziness and alarm. I knew that it was always like this that the problems started, and that shortly they would send me to bed, because I was no longer able to control them. I tried to accept the situation, but I couldn't manage it. My distress only got greater.

I thought that I ought to do something immediately, because in a little while I wouldn't be in a position to do anything. I got up from the chair, went into the kitchen, and, following the Master's recommendation, began to prepare food. I must admit that I had to press myself very hard to do it, and I certainly didn't do it with my mind and heart, but I managed to cook something – something very simple, of course.

Preparing the food gave me encouragement, and it also made me glad. I'd managed to do something which I hadn't done for many months. But the most important thing was that I'd started to feel better and I'd avoided the panic crisis. I had, that is to say, succeeded in transforming into a creative act the energy which would otherwise have led me to an increase in my fears.

At that moment I felt a strong desire to tell someone what I had done, but because I was alone in the house, I found an exercise-book and started to write. On the first line I noted the date. Below, I wrote down in detail what had been said with the Master, and what of that I had managed to put into action. Without realising it, I had begun my diary, which I have continued even up to the present, when I am preparing to publish this book.

Two days later, I did something which I considered very important. I agreed to go shopping with my husband, to shops which I knew would not have many people in them. I couldn't say that it didn't require great effort for me to stay in them. Indeed, as soon as we went into the first, I began to feel dizzy and then my heart started to race. But I said to myself immediately: "Ioanna, there's no reason for you to be panic-stricken, you were expecting these symptoms. One step each time is enough. And today you've taken a big step. Try to accept your problem and you'll feel better."

These thoughts brought me round somewhat. As soon as I felt my tension increasing again, I again thought the same thing. This method helped me to stay in the shops, without making a run for it. From then on I went with my husband when he went shopping. I'd made up my mind that I would try to expose myself to the situation which caused me fear, because until I understood what was causing my fears and the means of dealing with them, this was the only method which would help to reduce them.

A few days later, I agreed to go on a trip with my husband to a nearby beach. When I got out of the car, I felt dizzy and took hold of his hand to prevent myself from falling. I thought for a moment of telling him that we should get back into the car, but when I remembered my pleasure at having decided to come with him, and the promise that I had given to the Master and to myself that I would try to overcome my problems, I began to walk again. To begin with, my steps were not steady, because my legs were shaking, but, the more I walked, the better

I felt. I looked at the people and surroundings with less fear, and, moreover, there came a moment when I caught myself admiring the deep blue sea. This, of course, only lasted for a few seconds, but it was a step. Again I'd done something that I hadn't done for a very long time. However, the most basic fact was that, for the second time in a few days, I had been able to make positive use of the energy and power which I had within me and not let it increase my fear. The same evening I cooked food under less pressure.

After what I had achieved in these early days of my therapy, I wrote in my diary:

> "I'm glad that I have understood, up to a point, of course, what my problem is, and that I have taken the first steps towards solving it. Naturally, I still have great difficulty in dealing with my problems correctly and in accepting the good and the bad as aspects of life itself. I believe, however, that in time I shall succeed in this, by changing my way of thinking."

ANXIETY AND ITS CAUSES

The specialists define anxiety as a reaction of fear for which there is no specific source, but which is indefinite, and as a state of generalised unease and restlessness which is not linked to any real stimulus. It is a pathological phenomenon, because there is no specific threat, in contrast with fear, which is a natural defensive reaction of the organism when faced with an existent danger. A phobia can be regarded as something between fear and anxiety.

After a study of books and my conclusion that a very large percentage of the earth's population suffers from the illness of our times – anxiety – a question was constantly going round and round in my head. What is to blame for the fact that man in contemporary society, in order to get over simple things in everyday life, puts into action mechanisms as if his life were being threatened at any moment, in spite of all the disastrous consequences which this entails for his health, and for his very existence on numerous occasions?

The Master carried out an analysis on this subject for me at our very first meeting, as I have already said. When I explained my problem to him, he replied that the reason that it had arisen was that I was dealing with some things in a wrong way.

"We must embrace the negative aspects of life", he told me, "with love and with the mind, and not with the emotions, which create most problems. If you have difficulties in your relations with certain people, try to see them not as strangers, but as a part of yourself, as your own self."

"You have to realise that we all have our higher and our lower self. Just as, then, we forgive our lower self when it acts wrongly, we should, in the same way, be understanding towards others. No one is only bad. On the contrary, the nature of man is good. His erroneous behaviour is due to the ignorance in which he remains because no one helps him to emerge from it. Instead, therefore, of rejecting others for certain actions on their part, let us accept them with understanding, let us regard the actions as our own, and let us attempt to draw them out of this ignorance by the best means that there are, by love."

"But, Master, to analyse all these matters theoretically and to understand them is, up to point of course, relatively easy. But how can you apply them in practice? For example, how can I manage to solve my problems using the mind, reason, and love, the concept of which includes, as its most basic feature, acceptance?"

"In order to help you over this, I shall recommend that you carry out an exercise. You will close your eyes and you will imagine yourself to be in your infancy and crawling, using only your instincts, as animals do, in order to ward off dangers. And while you are at that age and crawling, you see wild animals coming into view in front of you to attack you and to tear you to pieces. You will have to either hide or face up to them, and, of course, because you are an infant, the only thing you can do is to hide. So if you stay at that age, all the time you will crawl, you'll be afraid to look at dangers, and you will be choked by fears, lack of nerve, and, generally, your emotions. There is only one solution if you are to be delivered from all this. To stand upright, not to hide, and using your mind, to look life in the face."

When, that same evening, I was alone in my room, and when I was writing down in my diary the teaching

I had received that day, what Jane Madders, a physio-therapist, says in her book 'Stress and Relaxation' came into my mind to confirm it:

"The human body possesses a marvellous unified mechanism which permits all its systems to adapt quick-ly to changing circumstances and the corresponding stresses, whether these occur within it or in the exter-nal environment. When life is threatened, the whole body prepares itself for intense activity. This reaction – 'fight or flight' – however, is suited to primitive man who lived with the threat of immediate physical danger, but is un-suitable for dealing with the stress which our civilisation brings with it. We react in the same way to overcrowd-ing, the trials of travel, the struggle for social recognition, sudden changes in our way of life, and difficulties in our personal relations. Such reactions can lead to a great many physical and mental disorders."

These words provided me with the confirmation I was looking for, and then I thought: "All I have to do is to try to do the exercise". I closed my eyes, relaxed my body, to the extent that I was able to do this at that time, and I imagined myself to be an infant and crawling.

Suddenly I saw in my imagination wild animals emerg-ing in the distance. My first, instinctive, movement was to hide in terror. No thought, of course, of facing up to them. As long as they were prowling round me I felt my heart beating hard, while my body was paralysed with fear. When in a little while the wild beasts went away, I began diffidently to emerge from my hiding-place. But I hadn't had time to leave it when I saw another herd of wild animals approaching from some way off. And again I reacted in the same instinctive way and thought only of how I was going to hide. This scene was repeated again and again! Each time, that is, that the danger passed and I dared to come a little way out of my hiding-place, a new threat would present itself, which I would deal with in the same way. By hastening to hide.

When I opened my eyes, I began to understand what the Master had explained to me, and I realised that up to then I had remained at the age of infancy as regards my emotional attitude towards life. It was always with fear that I looked at every danger and at every problem which presented itself. I acted only emotionally. It was emotionally that I tried to get over my mother's oppression, even when I married. It was with anxiety that I lived all my years at school and my years at university.

Later, it was in the same way that I undertook the responsibility of my job and the upbringing of my children. This attitude, naturally enough, led to illness. And I say 'naturally enough' because where else can dealing with everything – thoughts, situations, events – only with fear, distress, anger, or any other emotion lead someone? How long can you resist life itself? It's certain that you can't stand doing it for long. If you don't learn to deal with it correctly, you're doomed. A correct approach, as I had understood, means "I straighten out my body, look life in the eye, and don't hide from it, because one day it will find me and crush me". A correct approach means "I accept, in principle, everything, I don't resist things, and with my mind and love I try to find the best solution, working with all my powers to achieve it".

This was the initial theoretical approach on my part to my problems. But the first time that I attempted to overcome a difficulty by applying this method, I didn't manage it. It seems that putting into action what you have learnt is the hardest part.

One midday, as I was returning to the office, to which I had started to go again for a few hours, I found a lady from Russia waiting for me with her little girl, who was three years old. This lady was faced with a lot of problems, and in solving them she had asked for our help. Her husband had turned her out of the house and she had nowhere to live. So that midday she came to the office to tell us that her husband had met her in the street and had struck her because she refused to leave for Israel; but the worst thing was that he had threatened her that he would take the child away from her, on the grounds that she wasn't in a position to look after it.

All this she told us in tears, while despair was written all over her face. Naturally enough, before I had time to set my mind to work, a strong feeling of pity possessed me, while the thought that I couldn't supply a solution and anger at her husband's behaviour shattered me. My heart started to beat hard, my arms and legs went numb, and my stomach churned.

In the afternoon when we went home, the situation had worsened. I tried to apply what the Master had explained to me, but I found it impossible to concentrate. My symptoms became more acute, and, after a considerable time, I went and curled up on the sofa. Things were out of control. I was having another panic crisis.

Just then, God sent me Dionysis. As soon as he saw me shaking and looking like a frightened animal, he asked me: "Mother, would you like to speak to the Master?"

"Of course I would", I replied, "as long as we won't be bothering him; it's late."

"The Master, Mother, is available all the time to those who seek his help."

And so, in a little while I was speaking to the Master. I explained to him what had happened and how I was feeling. When I'd finished, he said to me:

"You will accept that what has happened had to happen. You will see the situation as a natural reaction of your self and you will think that it will pass, just as a child's common cold passes. But why have you allowed the problem to overcome you and haven't set your mind to work?"

"I couldn't manage it; the symptoms were very intense and I was possessed by fear."

"But the good sea-captain remains in control of the ship in a storm and in good weather. You have to know that your symptoms are awaiting the order from your mind to tell them they are welcome, but now they have no reason to exist. Then these too will go away, like a child's cold."

These words of his were as wise as they were simple. And so, as soon as I had put down the telephone, I began to think. The more I thought, the more I calmed down. Nevertheless, Dionysis made me get up from bed so that we could go out for a walk. It was late and very cold, and so he wrapped me in a blanket. As we were going down the stairs, my legs were shaking. But I held firmly on to his arm and managed to get as far as the street.

"Now, Mother", he said to me, "you'll straighten your body and walk as the Master has suggested. You'll tread heavily and confidently on the ground and your mind will give the order which your symptoms are waiting for - that now there is no reason, no danger, to justify their existence."

And, in fact, in a little while, after we'd been for a long walk, and by thinking about what the Master had told me, I began to be calm. When we returned home, I did the exercises I had learnt and succeeded in arriving at a state where I was capable of writing in my diary. I knew that if I managed that, calm would come to me. Among other things, I wrote that evening:

> "This evening, I learnt to cope with a panic attack, by accepting this state of affairs as a natural reaction on the part of my self which, however, is unnecessary, since there is no longer any reason why it should exist. When my mind gives this order, my symptoms recede and I begin to be able to control them.
>
> In addition, I realised for the first time the mistake I'm making with regard to the problems of my fellow-men. And this, as the Master says, consists in the fact that I act emotionally, I identify with them, and I'm not aware that I shouldn't want at all costs to provide the answer that I think is right, because this is given not by me, but by God, who judges that perhaps what seems good shouldn't happen at that moment.
>
> I haven't learnt, when I want to help others, to use my mind. Today, the pity – out of control – which I felt for the lady and the fact that I wanted at all costs to provide the solution which I thought right caused my panic attack. I must work in this direction, not to allow myself to act in this mistaken way."

When I read these analyses today, I realise that the instructions they include are no more than practical exercises to make me change my thoughts, because, as I learnt later, this is very important. Klairi Lykiardopoulou, in her book 'The Master' Vol.III, writes on this subject: "Desire, in the form of attraction or repulsion, is what 'colours' things and then takes the form of thoughts – very often negative. Somebody says, for example: 'This person is a nuisance' or 'There is no hope of improving society'. All these thoughts lend to a situation or to a person a static picture, a pattern, or a label."

And she goes on: "The Master, in speaking about this human characteristic, the need for the constant 'colouring' of things, events, individuals, and situations, says that in this way innumerable thought-forms are created, that is, thoughts which give a specific form to people, events, etc. Since the ordinary human being is governed by insecurities, fears, and desires, these thought-forms most of the time are negative, whether they concern himself or others. Humanity constantly has negative thoughts about a great many things, and then these affect everyone together and individuals also in a negative way, as in this way a strong emotional field, causing even greater tension in problems, is structured.

It is, in any event, a well-known fact that many illnesses arise from fears, anxieties, resistances, and unwelcome thoughts about health, thoughts which in the end have a negative effect on the body of man and which weaken him."

She then goes on to explain exactly in what way a negative thought-form has a negative effect and a positive thought-form a positive one – what in fact happens when a person gives form to an idea, whether or not he expresses it.

Ioannis Nestoros, in order to stress how much thoughts influence the individual, says in his book 'Composite Psychotherapy':

"It seems that Shakespeare knew this when he made Macbeth say: '...why do I yield to that suggestion / whose horrid image doth unfix my hair / and make my seated heart knock at my ribs, / against the use of nature? Present fears / are less than horrible imaginings'."

I now know that the reasons which caused the panic crises each time were many, and were due to the boundless gaps which I had, to my human deficiencies, some of which I still have, only now I know what they are. For the recognition of these gaps and filling some of them, time, effort, a definitive decision on my part that I wanted to get better, the help of the Master, and, above all, my faith that God would help me, not to rediscover, but to discover for the first time the strength to carry on with my life, not crawling, as I had done up to then, but with my body upright and treading firmly – all these were needed.

Before I end this chapter, I have to say that the panic attack which I have described above was the last that I experienced. And to think that only two months had passed since my discipleship started. Of course, I have had intense symptoms in some cases and my fears may, to a certain degree, sometimes visit me, but now I have learnt how to guide them and overcome them.

THE IMPORTANCE
OF RELAXATION

Relaxation and its importance for the acquisition of peace of soul was one of the first matters which the Master explained to me. "When this does not exist", he told me, "there is a retention of the soul's energies within the body, which creates anxiety and so we are involved in a host of illnesses. Calmness is the source of power. This is the reason why relaxation is taught to all the members of our Society in our groups for the study of the self.

When a person learns to relax, he begins to see life through new eyes, as something good, because the power of the soul which has been withheld finds a way out and becomes dynamic creativity. By relaxation, our mind is liberated and we cease to be possessed by emotions which give rise to tensions within us."

"And how can a person relax?" I asked him in a trembling voice, while my heart was nearly bursting from my chest. From the moment that he started to speak to me about relaxation and at the thought that he would tell me to do certain exercises, an inexplicable fear began to seize me, because I would have to do something unknown to me, and at the same time I said to myself: "Whatever you tell me, I'm not going to do it, because instead of doing me good, it may do me harm. Very well, I agree to having a conversation, because I take away from that what I think I need, but relaxation, a technique which I don't know – I'm not going to practise it."

"But it's simple", he replied. "You will sit comfortably in a position where the spinal column is straight, you will close your eyes, and you will think only of the specific task that you are carrying out at that moment. You will think of your body and the place where you are. You will let yourself calmly feel the weight of your body and you will follow your breathing. These things help in distracting your mind from other thoughts and emotions."

"The ability to relax", writes Klairi Lykiardopoulou in her book 'Spiritual Healing', "exists in every human being. As long as he doesn't have negative thoughts and doesn't doubt its importance." And I not only doubted it; I feared it. In the state that I was in, the one thing I didn't need was an extra fear. For the present, I had overcome this fear by my decision not to try out this technique. But I knew that the Master would come back to the subject and I had to do something about that.

From the next day on, I began to look for books on the subject, not in order to obtain confirmation for this teaching, since I believed that there were no such books, but in order to make my resolution on not practising relaxation stronger. So it was with surprise that I discovered that innumerable books have been written on the subject. I obtained some of these and started to read them.

All of them said that today many people are looking for natural methods to help to liberate their selves from hypertension. Recently, for the first time, serious research has been undertaken into the effectiveness of the methods which aim at the acquisition of this control. And it has been proved that the various relaxation techniques can significantly reduce the unfavourable consequences of prolonged anxiety.

It is true, they said, that anxiety and muscular tension go hand in hand. When a human being is in a state of stimulation and alertness, the muscles tighten, ready for action. And so, exactly as muscular tension is related to arousal and anxiety, so relaxation can bring about a feeling of calm.

I found scientific confirmation that relaxation does in fact reduce stress in man in Jane Madders' book 'Stress and Relaxation'.

In everyday language, the author tells us, 'stress' refers to the anxiety and alarm created by any charge, pressure, or difficulty.

In biology, the word 'stress' refers to whatever constitutes a real or apparent threat which would have an unfavourable effect on the organism. Nevertheless, neither of the above definitions conveys in a comprehensive way the meaning of the word as it is used in order to express a human state. The broad view of the subject, as described by the specialist physiologist Dr H. Seley in his book 'The Stress of Life', goes further. He defines stress as the rhythm of natural wear and tear of the body and shows that there is a general adaptive reaction, whether the factor which causes it was pleasant or unpleasant. Cold, he tells us, heat, anger, drugs, even unalloyed joy – all these set in motion the mechanisms of stress within the body in the same way.

There are plenty of reasons why we need to learn the technique of relaxation, Jane Madders tells us:

"It is a good way to overcome stress."

"It helps us to avoid unjustified fatigue."

"It raises the level of tolerance of pain."

"It enhances our personal relations. We get on better with others when we are relaxed."

"It improves bodily skills."

In conclusion, the author tells us that anybody can learn the techniques of relaxation and then apply them to everyday situations. It requires only some understanding, a little practice, and, above all, trust in the marvellous ability of the human body to heal itself, given the chance.

In looking for information in the books of Greek philosophers of antiquity, I learnt that our ancestors used relaxation as a preparation for thought, reflection, self-knowledge, and spiritual aspiration.

When I discovered that a great many people today practise relaxation, with very positive results, my fear and resistance of its practice on my part grew considerably less. So one day I decided to do the simple exercise which the Master had shown me. I shut myself in a quiet room, sat in an armchair, closed my eyes, and tried to centre my attention on my body and the place and to observe my breathing. A waste of time! To begin with, I had the feeling of complete darkness, and the next second my mind had left the work I was doing and had focused on my problems, with the result that I felt greatly disturbed. Disillusioned, I abandoned my attempt, and in order to calm down, I began to do the other exercises which I had been taught.

Now that I think about it, I realise that my resistance to relaxation was not due to my fear of practising something unknown to me and lying outside the methods of classic medicine, but to the following two reasons - of which, naturally, I was not aware. The first was the reaction of my personality against relaxing, because, unconsciously, I knew that through this exercise liberation of the mind occurs, its freeing from the emotions, self-observation, and that in this way its mistaken actions would be revealed – which I didn't want to happen.

The second was the fact that in my mind I had associated relaxation with Eastern religions. It was natural, therefore, that I should react in this way since I believed that if I accepted relaxation, I would betray my faith in Orthodoxy. This, it seems, was the reason why my resistance was reduced to a minimum after studying books by the Fathers of our Church; the spiritual wealth of these is very great.

My attention was greatly taken by what they write about prayer, which is the spiritual and mystic communication of man with God, by which our hope in Him is confirmed and demonstrated. All the Fathers teach that in order to be able to pray, we must be calm and with a good disposition of the soul.

At this point, it occurred to me that it is impossible to feel calm in the soul if bodily calm, which helps the individual to free himself from the tensions of everyday life and from the various thoughts which flood his mind, does not come first. And this is achieved by relaxation.

One of the books I read was entitled 'The Adventures of a Pilgrim', the author of which is unknown. It was originally written in Russian around 1853, and has been described as a masterpiece by European theologians. In this book, he narrates the way in which he succeeded in practising unceasing or mental prayer, or prayer of the heart. In this he was helped by a monk and the book 'Philokalia'.

At some point he writes: "One day, the elder opened the Philokalia and read to me the following from Symeon the New Theologian: 'Sit down alone in silence, lower your head, close your eyes, breathe calmly, and imagine that you can see into the depths of your heart. Make your thoughts issue from there in your heart, and, in time with your breath, say: Lord Jesus Christ, have mercy on me. Say this invocation with your mind, attempt to drive out any other thought, and advance.'

So I began to examine my heart in accordance with this teaching. With my eyes closed, I fixed my thought and my imagination on my heart. I tried to picture it and hear its beats. I began to do this several times a day, for half an hour each time, and to begin with, I felt nothing except a sense of darkness. However, little by little, for a very short time on each occasion, I was able to picture my heart in my mind and to follow its movements. After three weeks, I started to have, from time to time, various feelings in my heart and thoughts in my mind. I felt as if my heart were bubbling with joy, so great was the illumination, the freedom, and the consolation which were establishing themselves within them."

At another point, when he himself, as he tells us, had understood what interior prayer means, when he was teaching a Pole everything that he had learnt, he said to him: "The powers which we have within us slacken and disappear under the bulky weight of our material bodies, our material thoughts and cares. But when we concentrate and withdraw from everything that surrounds us and become more perfect, as if dematerialised, the soul returns to its true self and works with all its powers unfettered."

The conclusion I drew from all this quest was that relaxation not only helps to bring about bodily calm and to get rid of stress, but it is the first step in the spiritual progress of man towards God.

After coming to this conclusion, my fear of practising relaxation disappeared. In spite of this, I had great difficulty in implementing it in practice, and I may say that even today I do not manage to relax enough. This happens every time I pass into a state of separateness, every time that I shut myself in my ego again.

Fortunately, this occurs with less and less frequency, and I believe that the moment will soon come when it won't be necessary for me to do relaxation exercises in order to calm down and to think about how to deal correctly with life, with my problems, and with others, because now I have realised that the other person is none other than an extension of myself.

THE IMPORTANCE OF THE UNION OF MAN AND WOMAN

In one of the first meetings with the Master, while I was reading out my diary, he interrupted me and said:

"Mrs Ioanna, the way you speak is not correct. In speaking, your mind should play a part and it should be with emphases. Go on with the reading now, but try to make your voice as I have told you, so that it doesn't come out of your abdomen."

I went on reading, trying to correct my speech, but I didn't succeed. My voice continued to sound as it had before. I definitely needed time to alter my way of speaking, and, as I now see, a condition for that to happen was a change in my way of thinking and acting.

Nevertheless, my attempts at an accentuated and correct manner of speech, following the advice of the Master, helped in reducing the acuteness of my symptoms. I had noticed that every time that I was in a state of panic, my voice was breathless and it was only with difficulty that other people could understand what I was saying to them.

With the effort that I made to concentrate on my speech and to speak up, my symptoms became milder. In the early stages, Dionysis helped me a lot; when I spoke to him and my voice was not steady and loud, he wouldn't answer me. In this way he forced me to put the Master's recommendations into practice.

Little by little, my attempts to speak correctly became an exercise like all the rest which I was taught later. I can't say that this exercise in itself was a method of therapy, but after each effort, I felt less fearful and this was very important in the beginning, because in this way I became able, even for a little while, to think, to read, and to understand certain things. Later, I replaced this exercise with singing.

When I'd finished reading out my diary, the Master asked me:

"Do you sing, Mrs Ioanna?"

"I used to sing a lot, Master, and to do church chant, and I did it very well, but all this was before I was ill. In recent years, I've forgotten how to sing."

And then came what was a surprise for me. The Master started to sing in a wonderful voice, whose pitch made a great impression on me. When he'd finished, he said to me:

"You must sing; singing does you good. And chant, as well, since you like it. But you must sing with the larynx and not with the stomach, and your voice must be strong and you must give colour to it. Also, I would recommend that you choose the songs and music which you hear. Because if these have an intellectual content, then the higher centres are vibrated and the heart and mind are enlarged, that is, vibrations of the downward centres are avoided and so man is not identified with desires and emotions. And now I shall sing you a song, which I will then analyse for you." And he began to sing the following song in the way in which only he knew how to sing:

"The fair-haired boy of some beautiful girl one evening was taken to the bottom of sea by the gale. And the boat returned on its own, without the fisherman in it, empty without a rudder, from the deep waters."
"With its lamp out, one dark night it came into the harbour, the orphaned little boat. And all hopes were drowned in the deep waters, and the boat returned alone without the fisherman in it."

"This song", the Master explained, "tells us that the girl, though she ought to have really loved the boy, didn't love him. And instead of enclosing him in her heart, she drowned him in the deep waters, that is, in her emotions, in her belly, in the darkness. And the boat – that is, the body – returned on its own, with its lamp out, that is, without the boy's soul, which was light for the girl, in it. And so she herself remained in darkness, without light, for her emotions to drown her."

This interpretation of the song made a great impression upon me. I still didn't know that a large part of the teaching of the Society deals with the correct building of the relationship between man and woman. But since by this analysis it seemed that all the weight of this relationship falls on the woman, I asked:

"Is it only the woman, Master, who must love the man and not drown him in her emotions, in darkness? Shouldn't the man do the same?"

"Of course the same applies to the man as well. The man and the woman must enclose their partner in their heart, because it is only then that they will be enlightened by the light of the other, and will not live in darkness. But the woman, who by her nature usually acts more emotionally, must see her partner both as a man and as a small child whom she must nourish, and forgive his disobedience and misbehaviour, as she does with her children. It is the woman who by her love can make everyone around her happy. By giving her love unselfishly to all, she gives happiness to others – and also to herself."

I looked at him in silence and in great disappointment, because, according to this analysis, the only person responsible for the state of affairs which I'd reached was myself, because I didn't really love my partner, and this I could not accept. Reading my thoughts, he said to me:

"What's the matter, Mrs Ioanna? Don't you agree with what I've said to you?"

"But, Master, how could I agree? Am only I to blame for everything? Doesn't my husband have his share of the responsibilities? Doesn't he have weaknesses? Egoism?"

"Of course he also has weaknesses and faults; that is true of everyone. In the family, it is not angels or saints who are living together. Both the man and the woman are imperfect, since they live in ignorance. The difference with your husband is that he has accepted your weaknesses and your faults up to a point, which is something you haven't done, and you continue to resist, unconsciously, your own. And so you must, by analysing events on every occasion, become aware of what it is that bothers you, so that it will stop bothering you."

"But is it an easy matter for all this to happen?"

"No. It isn't easy. I would even say that it's very difficult. But it's not unattainable. And it's difficult because egoism creeps in between couples, putting forward its innumerable 'I wants' and seeking the satisfaction of its endless desires."

"But I have loved and still love my husband. Why has our relationship, from the day that I became ill, gone from bad to worse?"

"Because, quite simply, the love that you felt for him was not true, real love, which doesn't have limits and doesn't set up barriers. When you truly love, you accept the other person as he is.

But now you are called upon to find yourself through the trials you are going through. Because it is a trial which helps a person to find his balance in a world which is itself constantly in turmoil between disharmony and harmony. The whole of humanity has the same problems that you have. If you look around you, you will see that jealousy, insecurity, fear, and depression are phenomena common to mankind and not individual."

At this point what the Apostle Paul wrote in his Epistle to the Romans (5: 3-5) came to my mind: "Suffering leads to patience, patience to stability, and stability to hope. And hope in the end is not disappointed. Through suffering man acquires the knowledge which he lacks."

This was the first analysis which I had on the building of the man-woman relationship and its importance for their spiritual development. During the course of my discipleship, I heard very many analyses on this subject, and the acquisition of the most important good – love – on which the whole of the teaching of the Society is based, and which St Paul in his Epistle to the Colossians (3:14) calls the bond of perfection, that is, a link which unites and binds together all the virtues into a single whole. The person who loves has patience, kindness, does not envy, does not exalt himself, nor is he proud, but behaves decently, is not an egoist, and is slow to get angry. He who loves accepts everything. Faith, hope, and patience never leave him. St John Chrysostom says that love is the queen of the virtues. It is the medicine which cures all hardships of the soul and creates only mutual obligations and duties, and never superiority of the one over the other.

If, then, the importance of this unique virtue is so great as regards the relation of an individual with his fellow-men, it is easy to see its importance for couples. Because they are not merely very near to one another. They are 'one flesh'. They are a psychosomatic totality which is not separate and not divided. Here love must be 'the bond'.

When I had been convinced of the great importance of love in the right building of the relation between man and woman, I began my efforts to discover and draw upon my own reserves of love, in order to use them in improving my relationship with my partner.

I had been with my husband for some 38 years. We married after an affair which lasted eight whole years. We had two children, our son, Dionysis, and our daughter, Anthoula, and we lived happily, at least in the early years of our marriage. Later, some clouds appeared. But the situation became unbearable from the time that I became ill. I started to speak to him abruptly, and when he answered me in the same tone, I became hysterical.

I believed that time had wiped out his interest in me and for that reason he wasn't supporting me properly. This thought wounded me incredibly. It was impossible at that time for me to imagine that it was I and not he who had changed behaviour. Day by day the situation grew worse, to the point where I heard him, despairingly, tell our son that he could stand no more. I don't know where we should have ended up if my husband had not loved me very much and if our son had not seen to it that I should see the Master.

By means of the explanations which he gave me, I came to understand that the mistake was mine, and, consequently, it was I who must change so that my husband could change and express his love freely.

All my life I had got used to seeing his love and his interest through some of his actions, and I had never heard him express them to me in words. And all my life I used to say: "It's just his character, he simply isn't demonstrative". I had to be ill, to suffer, and to go to the Master to learn that I had first to let my love show itself freely, without expecting any return, for him to be able to do so himself.

Incredible though it may seem, within a very short space of time, things in our relationship changed so much that if I didn't sometimes have my symptoms tormenting me, I would have said that everything was as it had been before. And to think that at the beginning the change was not due to my having accepted my husband. I had simply come to a compromise with his negative sides and had persuaded myself not to resist them.

The teaching on the union of man and woman continued to cause me problems even after several months of discipleship. It was difficult for me to accept that if the man and the woman do not accept one another totally and do not interrelate their souls' characteristics, they will never be integrated people.

I didn't understand why an incomplete union between them is the reason which leads them not to accept people and, consequently, their own self, thus causing even mental illnesses in them. I didn't understand that as this union advances, the more that resistance to its realisation is reduced, the more union with others, acceptance of their negative aspects and of the negative aspects of life, goes forward.

I discovered at that period that if I could not find evidence on which to base this teaching, I should not be able to accept it, and, therefore, however much I tried to apply it, the result would be no more than a compromise solution. My next step was the search for that evidence.

OTHER VIEWS ON THE UNION
OF THE COUPLE

When I realised that I hadn't accepted the teaching about the union of man and woman, and that the change in my behaviour towards my partner was not the result of acceptance but of compromise, I reached the conclusion that if I didn't find information to check on this part of the teaching, every effort would be wasted. I knew that compromise would not help me for very long and would not bring complete peace if total acceptance and real union did not come.

The first books in which I looked for this information were the Old and New Testaments. And although I had been taught the texts of Holy Scripture – or at least a

part of them – at school and I hear them in church during the Divine Liturgy or during the administration of the
Sacraments, I realised for the first time that in order to
understand these texts, it isn't enough to read them and
translate them: you must be able to interpret them. Such
interpretations and analyses I found in many books by
modern theologians. N. Vasileiadis in his book 'Orthodoxy and Feminism' answers various burning questions
posed by contemporary society, and also deals with the
issue of the union of the two sexes.

"The Fathers of our Church", he writes, "in going more
deeply into the words of the Old Testament: 'And God
said, Let us make man in our own image, after our like-
ness: and let them have dominion over the fish of the
sea ... And God created man in his own image ... ; male
and female created he them' (Gen. 1:26, 27), came to
the conclusion that when God gave Adam 'the breath of
life' (Gen. 2:7), that embrace of divine love for His creature endowed with reason, Adam already had Eve within
him." And he goes on: "But since this matter is one of the
most difficult in Christian anthropology and requires a
great deal of theological training for an understanding of
it, I confine myself to citing the opinion of St John Chrysostom, who, in exploring the above two verses from Gen-
esis, says: 'You see how Holy Scripture by these words
suggests (in advance) the treasure which is hidden. Be-

cause the sacred writer, who speaks with the inspiration of the Holy Spirit, sees those things which do not yet exist as if they had already come to pass. By the words 'let us make man' it is clear that he is hinting at the 'creation of woman'. Because,' Chrysostom continues, 'whereas up to now he has not taught us about the creation of woman, he says 'Male and female made He them'. You see that he narrates the event which has not yet taken place as if it has happened. So when he has said 'Male and female made He them', He now gives His blessing to both, saying 'And God blessed them ...'."

And Vasileiadis continues: "We see, that is, that Adam, who had been created 'in the image of God', before Eve had been created, bore within him the archetypes of the female element. Adam contained in himself the male and female element undifferentiated. Furthermore, in Hebrew the word 'Adam' is a collective term. Consequently, at the moment when God called Adam into life, he already had Eve within him."

"In his homily, St John Chrysostom, in stressing that God always lays down 'common laws' which apply both to men and to women, even when He gives the impression that He is addressing Himself only to men, notes: 'For man and woman He knew as one living being, and nowhere divides the race'. That is to say, He truly regards man and woman as one being, as one human, and in no circumstances does He divide the race."

At another point he says: "The resourceful wisdom of God divided man into two at the very beginning. And wishing to show that, in spite of the division, he still remains one, He did not permit the one to be sufficient for the birth of children. Because he who is now is never one, but the half of one human being. And he concludes: 'so even now from one man is born'. Because the woman and the man are not two human beings, but one. And since 'neither man is without woman nor woman without man', this means that now that each is the cause of the life and existence of the other. And this contributes to the fact that they are a 'man and woman being'."

In conclusion, Vasileiadis writes: "As soon as Adam saw his wife for the first time, he welcomed her with a cry of wonder and an enthusiastic and lyrical song. He said to her: 'This is bone of my bones and flesh of my flesh'. That is, 'this creature, who has been formed in this way, is bone from my bones and flesh from my flesh'.

With these words he drew attention to the identity of his nature with hers and stresses that this is his other 'ego', because in many Semitic languages the expression 'my bone' is used instead of 'I'. These words of Adam confirm the organic unity of the two sexes, male and female, in one person. They confirm a fulfilment of one another and a close interdependence of the one on the other. If we see only man or only woman as autonomous creations, we do not have the perfect, the full, the integrated human being. So the Creator took one of Adam's ribs. And thus the man would have one rib of the human being missing, while the woman would be the other rib of the whole human."

Apart from religion, science also maintains, indirectly but clearly, the view that man and woman constitute one person. The psychoanalyst Carl Gustav Jung, in formulating the concept of the 'collective unconscious', includes among the terms which he uses those of Anima and Animus. Anima is the term which he gives to femininity, and the female part of the soul of each man, while the term Animus is the name given to masculinity, and the male part of the soul of every woman.

The ancient Greek philosophers also concerned themselves with the subject of the union of man and woman. In the Symposium of Plato we are told that when it was the turn of Aristophanes to speak about love, he began his speech as follows:

"First of all I must explain the real nature of man, and the change which it has undergone. For our original nature was by no means the same as it is now. In the first place, there were three kinds of human beings, not merely the two sexes, male and female, as at present: there was a third kind as well, which had equal shares of the other two, and whose name survives though the thing itself has vanished. For 'man-woman' was then a unity in form no less than name, composed of both sexes and sharing equally in male and female. [...] The form of each person was round all over, with back and sides encompassing it every way; each had four arms and legs to match these, and two faces perfectly alike on a cylindrical neck. There was one head to the two faces, which looked opposite ways; there were four ears, and double sex organs. [...] The creature walked upright as now, but also whirling over and over [...]. They were of surprising strength and vigour, and so lofty in their notions that they even conspired against the gods. [...]

Thereat Zeus and the other gods debated what they should do, and were perplexed: for they felt that they could not slay them like the Giants, whom they had abolished root and branch with strokes of thunder – it would only be abolishing the honours and observances they had from men. [...]

Then Zeus, putting all his wits together, spoke as follows: 'I think that I can contrive that men, without ceasing to exist, will stop their iniquity through a lessening of their strength. I propose now to slice every one of them in two, so that while making them weaker, we shall find them more useful by reason of their multiplication; and they shall walk upright on two legs.'

[...] 'So saying, he sliced each human being in two; and [...] he bade Apollo turn its face and half-neck to the section side [...] so that it might see it." And the poet continues his description of this division with details of how it took place.

But the point which is particularly noteworthy is where he tells us that after this division of our organism, each one seeks his/her other half and they go together. They wrap their arms around each other and remain in a tight embrace, filled with longing to become one again. And he concludes: "Thus anciently is mutual love ingrained in mankind, re-assembling our early state and endeavouring to combine two in one and heal the human flaw. [...] The craving and pursuit of entirety is called love. Formerly – as I have said – we were one; but now for our sins we are all dispersed by God. [...] What I mean is – and this applies to the whole world of men and women – that the way to bring happiness to our race is to give our love its true fulfilment: let every one find his own favourite, and so revert to his primal state."

Ioannis Sykoutris, in his book 'Plato's Symposium', writes: "Aristophanes' myth is of an anthropological character, and similar myths had been written by the pre-Socratic philosophers. In the view of scholars, beneath the comicality of the form of the myth, a content of deep thinking is apparent. In his speech, for the first time love is presented with its true nature, that is, as the great mystery and the great miracle of creation, which, for this reason can only be conceived mythologically. Here, for the first time, the power of love shines forth over and beyond the rationalising teachings of the sociologist and the scientist. In the depths of the mythical conception is the observation that man as an individual is not self-sufficient.

He needs the complement of the other sex, which will make him not only viable, but happy, because true happiness can only exist in the fulfilment of his nature, over and above his individual ego, but within the bounds of an ego broader than that which the poet presents to us in terms of myth by means of the double human being, a symbol now of the species in the perfection of its existence.

This is the union in which 'I' and 'you' are extinguished in a chaos of eternity from which another existence emerges strengthened, with an unbroken linkage of the two souls and two bodies – precisely those which the poet described to us symbolically in primeval people.

This union was presented to us as a gift of God, as a work of the divine love for mankind. If it is imperfect, if it is interwoven with pains and worries, with searchings and disappointments – and how could it be otherwise, since it is a therapy, a correction of an evil – it is nevertheless a ladder by which we draw near to the ideal from which our opposing conceit has cast us out. He sees our completion with the other half of our ego as very difficult. But to get as far as that is something, and is divine."

I then looked for information with which I could support that part of the Master's teaching which says that it is the woman who gives rebirth to the man, because she has the power given to her by the love with which God has endowed her to change the hardest of hearts.

This power of the woman was recognised by the Fathers of our Church. St John Chrysostom says: "Nothing is stronger than a devout and wise woman in regulating, directing, and governing the man, and in shaping his soul, as far as she wishes." Of course, the opposite also happens. Just as a wise woman reforms the man, an unwise woman can lead him to destruction.

At another point, Chrysostom says, addressing himself to the husband: "Your wife is for you a harbour. If the harbour is rid of winds and waves, you yourself and your whole family will enjoy great calm." In other words, he is saying that his peace depends upon his partner.

According to St Paul, the woman is "the glory of the man", because by her radiant and pure life she serves as a mirror which reflects the face of the man, which reveals it to the man himself, and so perfects him.

Vasileiadis, in the book quoted above, gives his view of the same issue. He says: "The events we experience day by day in our times confirm that the moral regeneration of the man is very closely bound up with the recrudescence of love. And we must admit that an important part of the burden of this recrudescence falls upon the shoulders of the woman, and particularly of the wife, who is called upon, by the grace of her charm, the delicacy of her manners, and her love to contribute to the 'rebirth' of the man, thus rescuing a love which is constantly becoming weaker. Furthermore, the woman possesses moral courage, intuition, self-denial, patience. She knows how to speak directly to the heart and to touch the most sensitive point of the soul."

Otto Rank, a philosopher and member of Sigmund Freud's psychoanalytical team, following his disagreement with him, sought and found a simpler explanation of the psychodynamics of neurosis. This was the trauma of birth. According to Rank, man experiences the ideal life in his mother's womb. His separation from this causes him a primeval Angst. And every desire of the individual to return to the first source of pleasure, the mother, will also cause him Angst.

This Angst creates in man a fear of life and, consequently, mental illnesses. In Rank's view, that is, man, since he experiences the most ideal life within the womb, unconsciously throughout his life wishes to return there. We see, then, that the only one who can rid him of this Angst is a woman, by making him feel, by the total acceptance of him on her part and by her love, that he is in fact again in the most ideal period of his life.

It would be a major omission on my part if at this point I didn't quote some extracts from Klairi Lykiardopoulou's book 'The Couple's Role in Contemporary Society', in which she has analysed in a unique way all the issues concerned with relations between the couple, including the matter of union. She writes: "The individual who has accepted the opposing currents and expressions of his/her partner is ready to accept all the negative parts of life in all its manifestations. The person who accepts the form of the body of the opposite sex has taken a substantive step towards the acceptance of all the bodies of mankind. The person who has accepted the weaknesses or the negative aspects of his partner has served a discipleship in the acceptance of negative situations everywhere. And, finally, the person who has accepted and worked for the improvement of the displeasing characteristics of the other and of himself can begin to work for the evolution of the whole world which surrounds him."

At another point she writes: "By means of the boundless devotion of a woman, a man will find this love inside himself, he will unite it with his own strength, in order to arrive at harmony. In the mind of man there is knowledge; there is also the unconscious need for love which will redeem power. There is the dynamic male and the tender female element which strive to intersect and become the sacred man-woman. When a woman is united with a man, she sees that now that she does not want anything, she has everything. She has all the aspects of the man within her."

When I arrived at the end of my quest for truth in the matter of the union of man and woman, I was now convinced that the Master's teaching on the union of the souls of the two sexes which leads man to deliverance is true from beginning to end.

THE DRIVING LICENCE

"How is it that you don't come to the Society more often, Mrs Ioanna, to involve yourself more systematically with what goes on here?" the Master asked me at one of our meetings some three months after the beginning of my discipleship.

"That is very difficult", I replied. "We live a long way from here, and I don't drive – I'm afraid to. Ever since I was 20, my husband has been urging me to get a driving licence, and he's never ceased, all the years we have been together, to insist on this. But it has been something that, when I thought about it, terrified me. I was afraid of knocking someone down. It's not myself I was afraid for."

"Your fear of driving, Mrs Ioanna, is your fear of taking the steering-wheel of life into your hands, and that's why you let your husband drive you. And even your fear of knocking other people down means a fear of expressing yourself to them, a lack of boldness in dealing with them, with the result that your emotions stifle you. I think that the time has come for you to get a driving licence."

During the days which followed my mind was constantly occupied with the analysis which the Master had given me in connection with driving. According to this, I ought to take the steering-wheel of life into my hands and to stand firmly on my own feet – or to stop crawling or carrying on living with my fears and insecurities.

The idea that I ought to go on living as I had been chilled me. But, on the other hand, I was panic-stricken at the idea of obtaining a driving licence.

"The Master can't possibly have meant what he said", I thought, "for me to get a driving licence at my age and, moreover, at a time when I'm tormented by so many phobias. I believe that in the end he'll find some other way of helping me to stand firmly on my own feet."

But it seems that I had miscalculated, because at our next meeting but one he said to me:

"You haven't told me, Mrs Ioanna, what you have done about your driving licence."

"You know", I replied, feeling numb, "I'll probably start lessons in a little while, although I think I ought to postpone them for a bit, because at present I have a lot of trouble with pains in the neck and the spinal column, and I also feel dizzy. In any case, I would like to have stopped taking the pills when I begin lessons. I take very few, of course, but I haven't stopped altogether yet. However," I went on, "I can start on learning the road signs."

"Nothing of what you say is of any importance, and the next time we meet, I want you to tell me what you have done about this matter."

When I reached home with Dionysis, I was seized with panic. "So that's that", I thought. "This is as far as it goes. The Master will stop concerning himself with me, because there's no way that I'm going to get a driving licence. But why is he being so harsh with me, when he knows that what he's asking of me is impossible for me to do? Up to now I've tried to put his advice into practice, and I've made a lot of progress, so why does he want all my efforts to be wasted, so that I go back to the state from which I started out? And so if he really didn't want to help me, why has he bothered with me for so long?"

"No", I heard a voice inside me say, "the Master wants to help you and that's why he's asking you to get a driving licence, which is something that will contribute to the whole course of your treatment, and it seems that he's sure that you can do it. At least have a try."

The following morning, the first thing I did was to visit the driving school, which belonged to an acquaintance of mine. When I had asked for the information about what is needed in order to obtain a licence, I took away the booklet of road signs produced by the Ministry of Transport. So I wouldn't leave myself any scope to have second thoughts on the matter, I began straightaway to collect the certificates needed, and the next evening I took them to the school. The lady to whom I gave them told me that I would have my first lesson in two days' time.

It would be untrue for me to say that both before the lesson and while it was going on I was only slightly disturbed. What I felt in reality was acute palpitations, dizziness, and distress, and it was impossible for me to concentrate, or for me to understand what the driving teacher was telling me. In order to excuse myself for my poor performance, I explained to him that in recent years I had had severe psychological problems, that I was afraid of cars, and so I asked him to be patient with me.

His reply was that he couldn't see that I had any problem apart from that of age, which was the reason why I would need a few more lessons than young people required, but he believed that, with a little effort of my part, I would succeed in obtaining a licence.

At my next meeting with the Master, he asked me: "What have you done about the driving lessons, Mrs Ioanna?" "Yesterday I had my first lesson", I told him, while I said to myself: "I simply received an extension of the termination of my meetings with you".

"And how did you feel during the lesson?" "Panic, naturally enough! I was shaking all over, and, as you would expect, I understood very little of what the driving teacher was saying to me."

"That doesn't matter; little by little you will overcome your fear, and in order to help you do this, I will give you a new exercise for you to do. You will stretch out your arm in front of you, you will clench your fist, and you will hold it for a long time in this position. And you will say: 'I can hold it in this position for as long as I like, because I have the strength within me and the will to do this which I derive from God and which is inexhaustible. By the same strength I can overcome my problems as well'."

During the days which followed, and for as long as the driving lessons lasted, before leaving home, I would do all the exercises the Master had suggested, to which I had added the one with my arm, as well as relaxation exercises. Day by day, I began to approach the car with less fear, and this resulted in my making some progress in driving. In the meantime, I took and passed the road signs examination.

Throughout the course of the lessons, not a day passed without my feeling some of my symptoms when I was driving. Of course, these were usually mild and lasted as long as the lesson did. But when sometimes they were more severe, I dealt with them in the way which the Master had indicated to me.

One morning, however, when I was halfway along the Athens-Lavrio route, I began to be seized by slight agitation, which, by the time we reached Lavrio, was out of control. My heart was racing, I felt faint, and I was shaking all over. I tried not to resist all this, but I didn't manage it. I was back in infancy.

Before we started out on the return journey, I heard the driving teacher say to me:

"Mrs Ioanna, sit in the passenger's seat."

"It seems that he's realised that I'm not feeling well", I thought. This gave me some relief, because the thought that I would have to drive for another two hours in the state I was in made me feel even worse. I slumped into the passenger's seat and we set out.

We had only gone a few kilometres and had just entered the national highway when he stopped the car on the edge of the road and said to me:

"Come on, now we're going to change places."

As I had no choice, I took over the driving seat, started the engine, and we set out. I held on to the steering-wheel tightly and said to myself again and again: "Ioanna, stop crawling, stand up straight and face the problem, since you know you have the strength to do so. It's a simple thing. Concentrate on the driving and everything will be alright."

With all these thoughts, but also because my attention was concentrated on the driving, I began to feel better. This was the most important thing, because everything becomes easier when my problem ceases to be my sole thought. Thus, when I arrived at the office, things were much better; and they became better still when I realised that it was two o'clock in the afternoon and that I had been driving for four whole hours. That day I wrote in my diary:

"So what was it which made me lose control of the situation, when just the day before I felt stronger than I had ever done in the past three years? Was I perhaps afraid that I would not be able to do such a long drive? Had I tired myself more than I should on the day before, or was it perhaps that when I heard the word 'Lavrio', I remembered one of the worst situations which I experienced two years ago?

At that time, we had my husband's sister, who lives permanently in America, staying with us. From the first day that she arrived in Greece, she tried, together with my daughter, to persuade me to go with them on one of their day-trips to the nearer islands. They believed that if I managed to do something of the sort, it would be an important step for me. My reply, of course, was in the negative, because I was afraid to go so far away from home. Finally, one day they managed to persuade me to go with them to the island of Tzia. They told me that we would go with our car as far as Lavrio, and from there with the ferry; that would take about an hour to bring us to the island.

Naturally enough, the night before I didn't sleep well. One moment I was thinking that I should not have agreed to go on this trip, however short it was, because I wouldn't manage it, and this negative thought made the symptoms which I felt more marked, but then the next moment, I was telling myself that I should have the courage to take the next step.

Next morning we set out on the excursion. As we were driving to Lavrio, my state was under control. But as soon as we went on to the ferry and it set off, things began to deteriorate, until when we were halfway there, I realised that I would shortly not be able to control the symptoms I was feeling. When we reached the island, I was in a hopeless state, and I lost all control when we discovered that we would have to spend the night there because there were no places on the only evening ferry going back. The efforts of my daughter and my sister-in-law to help me were in vain. I was not capable of listening to a word. My contact with my surroundings had ceased, because through my negative thoughts my problem had become so inflated that my mind was unable to conceive or work on anything else. In my mind there was only myself and my problem. And since at that time I did not know that the only thing which could help me to overcome the crisis that I was going through was for me to manage to concede a small place in my mind to a thought which concerned someone other than myself, I remained in the same state for 24 hours. Shut in a hotel room, with the feeling that time had ceased to flow, I felt that I had been condemned to breathe my last there. The situation began to be a little better when we returned home. There I always felt safe, because I had convinced myself of that."

From the following day, after I had understood what had happened on the Athens-Lavrio road, the lessons continued normally, until one afternoon the driving teacher telephoned me to ask me to go to the centre at Holargos, because I was to take my driving test. And within 20 minutes I was, with my husband, at the point which he had told us. I cannot conceal the fact that I felt tremendous agitation. But all the time I was waiting for my turn to come, I was thinking of the words which the Master had said to me many times:

"Man conceals within himself an inexhaustible power which he derives from God. If he doesn't discover this power or if he doesn't succeed in expressing it, he is lost, because the problems never end. It is like the cycles of life, where one ends for another to begin immediately." By means of all these thoughts, I managed to reduce my agitation and to pass the test successfully.

I went on with the driving lessons even after I had acquired the driving licence, because I didn't yet feel ready to drive on my own. However, the longer the lessons continued, the calmer and more capable of concentrating on them I felt. About this, I wrote in my diary:

> "In recent days, in spite of the fact that I am taking lessons and during the course of these I feel a little tension, when I return home, and as soon as I do the exercises which the Master has taught me, I calm down and all day can get on with my jobs, with reading, and with writing up my diary. It is obvious", I continue, "that little by little I am finding my strength."

In parallel with my driving lessons, I continued my discipleship with the Master. It was this which helped me to broaden my mind and to see life from another position and viewpoint. Thus, I started gradually to realise that it wasn't necessary for me to do the exercises which he had suggested to me so often, but above all that I should try to become a spiritual person. Through these efforts, a day came when I succeeded in doing what I had considered unattainable. I got into the driver's seat of our car and set out on my own for a drive.

A year after this major success, I wrote the following in my diary:

> "Approximately a year has passed since I got my driving licence, but my performance as a driver is not particularly special. I have great difficulties on roads with a lot of traffic, as well as at night, and always, when I drive, I feel some slight agitation. Perhaps I ought to bear in mind that I started on driving at an age when many people stop, and, what is more, at a period which was difficult for me. I think that it truly counts as an achievement!"

AGORAPHOBIA

Some three years had passed since my symptoms began and in that time I had been having pharmaceutical
treatment, and attempted, following the doctors' instructions, to cope with the situations which generated fear by
constant exposure to them. Because, as I have already
explained, apart from generalised anxiety, I was afflicted
with other phobias, of which the most tormenting was
agoraphobia, my efforts turned first of all towards curing
this particular phobia, as it was this which placed the
most limitations on my life.

The word 'agoraphobia' was first used by a German
psychiatrist, Westphol, a hundred years ago, in order

to describe "being unable to walk in certain streets or squares". Today it is used to describe fears of being in public places, such as streets, shops, and enclosed areas.

This phobia afflicts approximately 6% of the world's general population, according to the statistics, with a great preponderance of women (approximately 80% - 90%), the majority of them married. So, in implementing a programme of desensitisation which I had drawn up on my own, I started to go to the shops in my neighbourhood, and within the space of two months I'd managed to stay there for as long as possible without being seized by a panic attack.

One morning I accepted the invitation of a friend to go with her to Kifissia for some shopping. To begin with, things went fairly well, but as time passed, I began to experience the familiar symptoms – which I thought that I had overcome. I followed my friend into the first shops she entered, but soon it became impossible for me to go into them and I waited for her outside. After the dizziness and palpitations, I had the feeling that I was going to faint, and the only thing I wanted at that moment was to be in the 'security' of my home.

Unfortunately for me, my friend had made plans for us to eat out, and so, when she had finished her shopping, she said we would go and sit in a restaurant. I explained to her that I was not feeling well and I asked her to postpone the meal for another time. But she, in an effort to help me, insisted, and I, having no choice, followed her.

About two years have passed since that day, and I still remember the sufferings I endured while I was in the restaurant. Each minute which passed seemed like an age. I shook all over and was bathed in sweat. When my friend saw that I couldn't even taste my food, she realised that her efforts to help me that day would have to stop, and, without finishing her meal, she said that we should leave. This incident was the cause of the unease which I felt for a considerable length of time each time that I went to Kifissia to shop.

In analysing various events which took place during the time when I was working to rid myself of my agoraphobia, I reached certain conclusions. First of all, I realised that exposure to the situation which made me afraid helped me to overcome my fears, to the point where I dared to confront them. I resolved one day to go to the nearest shop in my neighbourhood, and, when I repeated this ten or 20 times, I was then able to go to it and feel only slight unease.

Later, I tried to go to a shop a little further off, and so on. Each time, that is to say, I extended the circle within which I was able to move with relative ease. The problem, however, persisted and made its appearance as soon as I decided to move outside the familiar circle. I realised that this particular method was helping me only a little, and it was not liberating me from my phobias and from the restriction on my life. Liberation began to come much later, and only through the teaching I was receiving.

On the issue of fear, the Master says: "Are you afraid? Find out what it is you are afraid of, why you are afraid of it, and when you find out, you will cease to be afraid." Within those words lies the means of definitive healing. Naturally, 'find out' is an expression which is followed by thousands of questions, such as: 'Where am I to look?', 'What am I to look for?', and you can't get answers to these questions unless you have some guide to this searching of your soul, and, the most important thing of all, unless you decide to be honest with yourself.

But, again, no one should think that phobias and insecurities vanish as if by magic as soon as you start to follow a teaching. It needs time, and firmness in your decision to undertake continuous work.

At one of my meetings with the Master, I asked him to make me a deeper analysis than those which he had made up to then of the causes of phobias, and particularly of agoraphobia.

"Agoraphobia", he told me, "is a mental illness. People who suffer from it experience fear when they are outside their homes, in open or enclosed spaces and among people."

In answer to my question as to why the agoraphobe feels less fear when he is at home, he replied that man has associated his home with the place where, when he returns after the trials of the day, he finds peace and security, he forgets his problems and calms down. In this way, when he enters it, having convinced himself of the security which it provides, he begins to be at peace. He thinks that he has left his problems and fears outside the house. However, these are not solved by driving them out of your mind for a little while, but by dealing with them. Because if you don't do this, you will be constantly possessed by the same fears and by the same insecurities.

At this point, I couldn't help thinking that what the Master was telling me was entirely true. I knew from personal experience that my symptoms began one day when I was among people and were more intense when I was a away from home, whereas when I returned there, I was calm.

However, little by little, because, in my ignorance, I was not working on the recognition of their causes, the symptoms became equally acute even when I was at home.

To begin with, it was only the visits of certain people that I did not want. But soon, when the doorbell rang, I didn't want anybody to be there. I wrapped myself in the bedclothes, because I had started to tremble, as though the visitor was threatening my very life. Gradually, I came to want to see only the members of my family, but I couldn't sit down to eat with them at the table, because, it seemed, I couldn't stand even them. At that time I didn't yet know that the one I couldn't stand was myself! I couldn't accept myself, and it was this non-acceptance which was bringing about all my phobias.

These thoughts were interrupted by the voice of the Master, who was asking me what else I wanted to know about agoraphobia.

"What else, Master, but to know what these fears are due to, what causes them."

"Fears are due to the fact that man does not accept his good nature, the nature which God gave him. He doesn't recognise the good, and sees the good itself as evil. Thus he can't cope with all the emotions which others impose upon him, or with those which he creates himself, and which are often very heavy. He can't stand them and they often make him ill, because he hasn't the good in his mind, and consequently colours them as evil.

He sees the acts of others and on the basis of these, he divides others into good and evil and for this reason cannot stand them, just as he cannot stand himself, precisely because he is not in the truth, in knowledge, and suffers from ignorance."

"That is to say, does the fact that I am made ill by the problems of others mean that I am not in the truth?"

"Naturally you are not in the truth – out of ignorance, of course, since you don't see it."

"And what is the truth?"

"The truth is eternity, total health, absolute balance, pure knowledge and spirituality. The truth is a way of life, it is breathing, it is life itself. The important thing is to see where we are living, in the good or in the evil? What are we choosing? If we choose the good, we are always alright, nothing bothers us, and whatever comes to us becomes good. If we choose the evil, not in the sense that we ourselves are evil, but in the sense that we attach emphasis and importance to it, we are in the evil and we cannot escape from it. The negative features of life do not exist in order to cause us unhappiness, but to help us to learn to deal with them with a cool head, to become stronger, and to emerge from ignorance. You see how simple things are."

"Everything is simple, but everything is also difficult."

"Nothing is difficult. It is purely a matter of positioning the mind. What we call well-being, deeper spirituality, reflection are none other than the co-existence of two opposites, good and bad, man and woman, negative and positive. The mistake is to see only the one, isolated. It is like seeing only half of life. When we see the good within us, then we accept that what is regarded as evil is necessary, like the manure which is needed for flowers to grow. Without manure, flowers don't grow. Similarly, without the lower moments, without the lower intellect, there is no higher one, or higher spirituality. Man has constantly to remember his good nature, and not let the evil intrude. Because then we are not within love. We are within hate, we are within the half. Love is the whole. What, then, is the good, to sum up? The truth. What is the truth? The whole."

"Do you mean, Master, that for us the word 'lie' should not exist?"

"Yes, because a lie is the truth which man has made into a lie."

"However, we started this analysis from my question about what happens when others come to lay their problems upon us."

"It depends upon where they come to lay them. If they come to lay them on the evil, things are bad. They will be ill and so will we. If they come to lay them on weakness, things are difficult. If, however, they come to lay them on the good, on the truth, they are immediately assimilated. We must see things in their original nature – that is, the good. When the mind refers itself to that, the transmutation takes place at once. If, for example, we take a diamond and throw it into dirty water, will anything happen to it? Of course not. This is the good, and it is to this that everything must be referred."

So this is the point at which we arrived. The cause of phobias is the non-acceptance of the negative aspects of life, and of the negative sides of others, which results in the non-acceptance of our own self, since others are none other than an extension of ourselves.

At the same moment, the teaching of our Church, that we should love our neighbour as ourselves, came into my mind in support of the analysis which the Master had just made. Because what else is this commandment saying to man but that he should not separate others from himself, or classify them into good and evil, but should forgive them, as he forgives himself, and as God forgives all men?

Our ancestors were among those who have concerned themselves with the goodness of man's nature. Isn't the conclusion of Socrates, arrived at after many years of enquiry, to the effect that 'no man is willingly evil', telling us the same thing? Within those few words Socrates encapsulated a whole philosophy. When someone has understood the importance of these words and succeeds in applying them, he has embarked on the road to knowledge of the truth and all that remains is for him to work towards the total conquest of it.

The person who does evil to others, deep down, does more evil to himself. Because, according to the moral law of justice, sooner or later, he will be paid back accordingly. Consequently, no one is evil because he wishes to be, because no one wants to do evil to himself.

There are no good or evil people; there are people who know and people who do not know. And those who know must help the others to learn. By this approach, our behaviour and our mental health change completely. We do not condemn, we do not reject, we do not despise anybody. We accept everyone and love them. This is what the teaching of the Master says. Everything is of the nature of the good – all thoughts, all actions, all events, as long as they are assimilated into their original nature, into the truth, and do not become sickness.

All these analyses and thoughts led me to do a lot of thinking. I had understood the theoretical part, and I was convinced that it was correct, but I found it impossible to apply all these things in practice. I had the same difficulty in putting into practice the whole of the teaching, about one part of which I continue even today to have the same problem.

It is extremely difficult when an individual undergoes trials for him to see the good behind these trials – to accept, that is, the suffering and to think that this is no more than a part of life, which, taken as a whole, is a miracle. I, for example, when I have to deal with some problem of my own or of a fellow human-being, cannot assimilate it to the concept of the good. On the other hand, I have improved my relations with those around me, because I have succeeded in seeing that their negative aspects are only a small part of themselves, of their true nature, which is good. If they do not express this good nature, this is owing to the fact that they do not know that it exists within them, because no one has helped them to find this out.

A considerable time had passed since my discipleship began, and my health had very greatly improved when, one evening at a time of reflection, I was trying to remember some of the trials which I had been through in my life and to work out how I could have dealt with them in such a way that, instead of their making me ill, they would have been a cause of my spiritual evolution.

I went back to the time of my latest and long-lasting trial. The last three years and everything I had experienced in them passed before my eyes like a cinema film. I lived again my phobias, the panic attacks, my isolation from people, my visits to the psychiatrists, and, finally, my complete abandonment of myself to despair when I was convinced that no one and nothing could help me. And yet, in that time of despair, God sent His help. He led me to the Master, and my salvation began.

The analyses, the questions, the answers, and the conclusions sprang up, one after the other, in my mind. "So there is the good. The trials that you went through were the only way for you to seek out the truth. The proof of this is the fact that while you knew of the existence of the Society and had visited it, you didn't want to attend the teaching.

Or, rather, you didn't even think of it. You were, you see, comfortable in your egoism. In these cases, the only way for God to help man is to shake him up through a trial. And you ought to thank Him for that and because He helped you at the last moment to find the strength to go on with the battle of life."

ACCEPTANCE

The word 'acceptance' was one which I heard from the Master at our first meeting, but also the word which I never ceased to hear at all the subsequent ones. "Accept your problems", he told me: "And accept people, as well, because that's how God created them."

That day, I hadn't understood the great significance of this word, just as I hadn't understood how it is possible to accept pain, illness, one's problems, and, generally, all the negative features of life.

All this seemed to me unattainable and unrealistic. I couldn't imagine how it was possible when I was para-lysed by fear, to tell myself not to resist this, and so immediately to feel better. I had not understood that this stage is the apex and that, in order to reach that point, you are called upon to build it on your own by working hard.

However, as I have already said, the scope for my cure had narrowed a great deal and the Master was my last hope. And the first thing that he asked me to do was to accept my problems, and to do the same in my relations with others.

At the beginning of my discipleship, acceptance helped me very little, since I was unable to apply it. But the teaching on this concept continued. I heard many times that whenever I was seized by a symptom, I should set my mind to work and say that this was a situation which, whether I liked it or not, existed. If I accepted it and didn't resist, my mind would be liberated from the negative thoughts themselves and would begin to function, in order first to discover the cause of it and then how to deal with it.

Furthermore, acceptance is the first spiritual principle, and if that doesn't exist, there is no basis on which the other spiritual principles, the most important of which is love, can rest. How am I to love my problem if I don't accept it? Or how am I to love someone if this has not been preceded by my acceptance? The word 'acceptance', naturally, does not have the meaning of receptivity to everything passively and without further discussion. 'I accept' means I accept everything, positive and negative alike, but I constantly take action to set these things in order.

When I realised that I was unable to accept my illness, I decided to practise acceptance in my relations with my family. I put this decision into action immediately. Here I must explain that for the three previous years the situation in our home had been far from pleasant. I quarrelled with everybody and everything. I found fault with everybody, and the only person who was not at fault was myself. There were clashes of Homeric proportions when the others said or did something that I didn't like. Perhaps sometimes I had right on my side, but I voiced my view in such a way that it made them react against it. At the end of each quarrel, naturally enough, my state worsened and my family felt responsible for this.

My behaviour towards the members of my family changed radically as soon as I began my discipleship. I stopped raising my voice, constantly wanting others to do what I wanted, and I tried to please them by cooking something special, even if that required a major effort on my part. The most important thing was that I tried not to react with angry words to what they said or did that I didn't like. To begin with, they regarded me with some distrust. They couldn't believe in such a change – with the exception of my son, who attended my learning process. They didn't believe that it was possible for me to change so much from one moment to the next. They thought that all this change was due to some remission in my illness, and that in a few days I would go back to my old ways. But this didn't happen and the improvement in my behaviour continued.

Now that I think about the matter, I see that in the early days my change was not a consequence of 'acceptance' as taught by the Master – that is, as an accepting approach towards everything, through the reflection that all things, both negative and positive, are necessary for the whole, are parts of the manifestations of creation, and have as their purpose the broadening of consciousness through the stimuli to which they give rise.

My change was due to a compromise which I had reached over what the Master had asked me to express. I knew that if I didn't show a will to apply what he was teaching me, he would stop concerning himself with me, because from the first day he had told me: "We, Mrs Ioanna, don't force anyone to follow and implement our teaching. We give our help only to those who really wish to acquire knowledge which will enlighten the mind and will fill their heart with love."

Over and above my deeper motivation, it was the change in my behaviour which helped me to begin to be calm and to think. And the more I calmed down, the more this calmness was communicated to others. I didn't believe that my new attitude would bring about such a difference and so much joy to my loved ones. Things which only a little while before they had obstinately refused to do they now did of their own accord, without my asking them, simply in order to please me.

A beginning had been made, and the first results served to strengthen even more my decision for knowledge.

As the Master says, the cause of evil for man is his ignorance, which hides behind his negative stance towards unwelcome phenomena. Because what else could non-acceptance of the temporary nature of phenomena and of the fact that none of the things which surround us is eternal and unchanging be? Thus it is that at the thought of some loss we are possessed by fear, with all the consequences brought about by the emotions, which are not the result of reasoned thought.

And isn't non-acceptance of the truth that a negative aspect of others is none other than an aspect of ourselves, since in everyone there are all the aspects of life, a result of ignorance? Consequently, in not accepting these aspects, in essence we are not accepting our own selves and are involved in mental disturbances.

"And yet, Master", I asked him on the day when he was explaining these ideas to me, "is it possible for man to expand his mind to such a degree that he accepts everything – the positive and the negative – equally, and to open his heart enough for him to embrace everything without making distinctions?"

"Of course it is possible! Because deep within him man has a great need for union. The soul seeks to create a substantive relationship with others without reservations, but in this endeavour it is hindered by the personality. Thus the obstacle to acceptance is the personality, the chief characteristic of which is the retention of individuality. If we know the personality for what it really is, we shall be led to self-knowledge, which is the first element in the acquisition of acceptance. An individual who knows and accepts his own negative aspects becomes more accepting of the aspects of others."

"And how can one be brought to self-knowledge?"

"By observation. You begin to observe your self through the mind and to go more deeply into it."

"Yes, but man sees only the positive features of his self and doesn't want to see the negative ones."

"That is the work which he is called upon to do if he wishes to be delivered from the bonds of his ignorance."

At this point I remembered what Pythagoras had said: "When you go to bed, before you close your eyes, carry out an examination of yourself: What have I done today? What haven't I done? What should I have done?"

With the help of the Master's analyses and with his guidance, I began to observe myself, and by this work I brought to the surface my negative manifestations.

First of all, I noted that, up to that time, in all my actions I was led by my emotions, and it was with these that I approached the deaths of my loved ones, as I have already said. And, of course, not only with the feeling of sadness because they were cut off from life, but, above all, because I would be cut off from them. But what shattered me, and what I believe overwhelms everybody in these cases, was my unconscious fear of my own death, of the loss of my own form. And because this fear was unconscious and I didn't know about it, I was unable to reflect that death too is a part of life, and that if we do not accept this, the pain of loss becomes unbearable and fear of our own death can lead to madness.

What helped me at least to reduce my fear was the thought that God, who with unbounded love created man, couldn't have imposed death upon him only in order to cause him boundless fear and pain. "God is love", Scripture tells us, and everything He has created can only be a manifestation of this love. If therefore, we dwell on this simple thought, we shall at once come to the conclusion that death is none other than an expression of the Love of God. If, of course, we do not wish to see this boundless love, it is natural that we shall face death with fear and despair.

I also made this mistake over my illness. Every time that I experienced my symptoms, instead of accepting them, I resisted them, so that I ended up with panic attacks. And this was because I was afraid that in the course of such a crisis I would have a heart attack and die. I had not understood what Mrs Klairi writes: that if we suffer from pain, distress, and illness, this is due to the fact that we haven't realised what we are: a part of the miracle of God. Since, therefore, we are not aware of this truth, it is natural that we should not give expression to it, and should believe that for sorrow to become joy and sickness health is beyond our jurisdiction, beyond our self. But this is a mistake, because our self has the power to perform the miracle every second and to make illness health.

Little by little, and with the help of the Master, I began to use my mind, to change my thoughts and to make them positive instead of negative. Whenever I began to feel ill, I would say: "This is a situation which has come, and, if you accept it, in a little while it will pass. I must think of what the Master has told me – that I can become as strong as I am frightened now.

All that is needed is that I should believe this and never forget it. Man possesses will and strength within him and can intervene by means of these and guide his mind. Whenever an idea overwhelms him and gives rise either to positive or negative thoughts, he should call to mind the exact opposites, and so balance will come. Because even the positive, if it isn't checked, can cause imbalance."

All this I began to accept, of course, little by little and with great effort on my part – but chiefly by the undeviating position adopted by the Master. He would talk to me for hours on end in order to get me to understand something. He never stopped the teaching unless he was sure that I had understood the analysis which he had carried out. "We'll stay here until morning, Mrs Ioanna", he said to me one day, "until you understand what it is that I'm telling you."

It was natural that I should have difficulty in understanding all these analyses, as it was that I should often react against them, since, as my discipleship advanced, I realised that behind myself there was another self which I ignored and kept imprisoned and which, in its efforts to free itself, caused me confusion and trouble. I was greatly helped by reading the books on the subject.

In her book 'Anxiety, Depression: Prevention, Cure', the journalist Mary Tsolaka writes: "Thoughts have such power, such influence, that the brain is dynamically activated, that is, it comes to life so much that it cannot but channel this energy somewhere. From a scientific point of view, negative thoughts affect the circulation of the blood, whereas this in its turn affects all parts of the body, and so nourishment does not take place normally. Result: the blood is impoverished in constituents. When this was first heard of, many people made fun of it, because they couldn't believe that the mind has so great an effect on the body. Today, scientific research has been carried out which proves not only its influence on physical health, but provides the foundation for mental therapy."

At another point she says: "Our brain is a computer; whatever programme you give it, it will process it to perfection. If this programme is right, all is well: if it isn't, we will be tormented by a range of psychosomatic disorders."

The poet John Milton claimed that the mind of man can make a paradise out of hell and a hell out of paradise.

But what puts best the importance of positive thoughts is what Epictetus said: "Take more care to put evil thoughts out of your mind than to heal the sicknesses of the body".

The conclusion to be drawn from all this is that to be in good health, apart from anything else, the most important factor is our mental state. We must be optimistic, fearless, joyful, calm.

On the subject of thoughts and their importance, the Master says: "Man's greatest enemy is his negative self. It is this that first must change, for him to be really able also to change the conditions which oppress him."

Ioannis Nestoros, at some point in his book entitled 'Composite Psychotherapy', analyses the following text from Homer's Odyssey:

"It is in truth a shame that men blame the gods because they believe that disasters come upon them from us, whereas they suffer as a result of their thoughtlessness, without their fate being to blame."

"I think", he comments, "that Homer, by the words 'as a result of their thoughtlessness' is proposing something which forms the backbone of normal and pathological human behaviour. Human beings suffer because they think in a wrong way." In the same book, the author tells us that the psychotherapist R.D. Chessik considers that Socrates was the founder of psychotherapy. Socrates, relying on a specific method of discussion, maieutics, or 'midwifery', helps his interlocutor to arrive at the solution to his problem. The individual, by discovering the solution on his own, is convinced of his ability to do so. And he ends the chapter with the saying of Hippocrates – that the "physician-philosopher is equal to the gods".

In parallel with my study of these books, I continued to observe my reactions. I had noticed, for example, that in the early stage of my discipleship, although from morning till evening I felt quite well and was willing, without pressuring myself unduly, to go shopping, for a walk, or on visits, at night I decided not to leave the house. About this fear, I wrote in my diary:

"I think that the night-time affects me and produces unease in me because I react, uncon-

sciously, to the darkness, which expresses the negative aspects of life. I have not managed to regard light and darkness, the positive and negative, man and woman, and so on, as one."

Thus, when, one evening, my husband asked me to go out to sit somewhere and have a soft drink, I refused to go with him – in a categorical manner – because at the mere hearing of his proposal, I began to feel agitated, but this feeling disappeared as if by magic when I refused. This fact worried me and I began to study it.

First of all, I established that with the mere thought of going out at night I became agitated. That is to say, the thought of facing a situation of which I was afraid set in motion the mechanism of 'action or flight' from the situation which gave rise to fear, and I had chosen flight. Therefore, I thought, it's in my hands, or, rather, in my mind, to choose action, to face up to what I fear. And, just as on my refusal to go out with my husband, my fear and my symptoms passed off, I can, in the same way, according to the theory of the 'action or flight' mechanism, by changing my thoughts, deal with the situations which frighten me.

My second realisation was that I was still persisting in acting emotionally, and allowing my fears to limit my life. After these thoughts had passed through my mind, I jumped up and began to get ready. My tachycardia and dizziness made their appearance again, but their intensity was much less than before, and I tried to accept the situation, whereupon my resistance was reduced. I told myself again and again what the Master had recommended that I should say in such situations. "It is natural for you to react in this way, since you think that you are faced with some danger. But now that the danger has passed, you can calm down." And in fact, in a little while, I felt much better.

When we left home for our outing, the weather was very bad. There was a high wind and it was raining – sometimes snowing. In spite of this, we got into the car and went down to Rafina, where we went and sat in a café, which was fairly crowded. We ordered orange juices and began a conversation, just as in the good old days. Throughout our stay there I felt slightly uneasy and had palpitations, but this didn't stop me from staying for more than an hour. When we returned home, I wrote in my diary:

> *"This evening I feel very glad because I have managed to overcome my fear of going out at night."*

Another event to do with acceptance was the following: one morning, an old family friend called on us. He was talking to my husband while I was cooking in the kitchen when I heard my husband say to him: "Why don't you stay for a meal, as you're on your own at home?" I was immediately seized by disquiet, and at the same time I was thinking: "My God, how shall I manage to stay for so long with our friend? Why did my husband suggest that he should stay without asking me?" The situation couldn't be changed, because our friend had already accepted the invitation.

Given this situation, I began to think about and look for the cause of my agitation, so that I would be able to keep it at a low level. I saw at once that up to the moment when the proposal was made to our friend, I had been calm and his presence had not caused me any distress. I believed that his stay in our house would be short, since he'd come for a cup of coffee. The fact that I had arrived at the point of accepting friends at home, even for a little while, without this causing me acute symptoms, was very positive, it was a major step forward.

Then I began to think what was really happening to me. "Why, as soon as I heard that our friend was staying for a meal, was I seized with agitation? It seems", I concluded, "that acceptance had not advanced far enough. And in this particular instance, I did not accept two things. The first was that I would have to stay with our friend for some time, and the second that I was not asked by my husband about this invitation, which is something he has done all our life. It was natural, therefore, that I should be disturbed.

But is it right to invite people without asking me? No, it isn't right. But now the invitation has been issued. I can't take it back. The only thing I can do is to accept the situation, and when our visitor has left, have a quiet conversation with my husband. Of course, this conversation had taken place on other occasions, but always started out with my resistance to this aspect of him, and was doomed in advanced.

But was I perhaps thinking in a superficial way? Should I perhaps analyse his need for company? Perhaps this is so great that, in order to obtain it, he chooses to quarrel with me after the event? But why should he feel like that when I'm with him all the time?

The Master had told me that when we want or don't want something very much, something is going on and we have to look for that 'something'. In this case, I believe there can be many reasons. The first and most fundamental, in my view, is my own rejection of certain of his aspects, and he is aware of this. Unconsciously, therefore, by keeping company with his friends, on the one hand he's looking for their acceptance of those aspects of himself which I reject, and on the other, for the strengthening of his own position in order to deal with his unconscious enemy – myself.

A second reason may be the existence of certain gaps of my own, of which, also unconsciously, he is aware.

119

And so some of these he consciously manifests by his great need for company, as he believes that in this way he will fill them. In any event, it is certain that my non-acceptance will not help either him or me to overcome our problems. I must, therefore, accept the situation, I must have a conversation with him again, and wait to see the results, because complaining and quarrelling do not help with the solution of the problem."

By having all these thoughts, I succeeded in calming down. Preparing the meal and looking after our friend happened without my realising it.

The more acceptance advanced, the more things I managed to do. I had started to go to banks, to public services, to stand in queues, and on most occasions I succeeded in this without much agitation.

Moreover, one day, while I'd worked from morning to evening in the office and outside it, when we returned home, we found the electrician waiting for us, because we had a problem with the washing-machine. I told him what was wrong with it, and I was very pleased to note that whereas in the past in such circumstances I had been greatly upset and had gone to bed, this time I was dealing with the matter as though there was nothing wrong. I had accepted that this too was a situation which I had to deal with, so that the next day I would be able to wash the family's clothes. This day was a day of surprise for me.

However, the relative calm in the early days didn't last for long. The following afternoon, when I had visited a cousin at her home, where she'd returned after having an operation, while I was returning on foot to the office, I was suddenly overcome by dizziness and a disturbance of the heart and stomach. My first thought was to try to find a taxi to take me to the office. I was looking again, after some time, for the security of the familiar place in order to feel better. But I realised at once what it was I was going to do, and, recruiting all my forces, I stood still on a corner of the street in order to recover and to manage to think.

The first thing I tried to do was to discover the cause of my indisposition. I soon reached the conclusion that hidden behind my feeling unwell was again my fear of possible illness. I realised that I had not accepted this fear on my part, and so sometimes – like today – I expressed this through the familiar symptoms. Now, however, I knew that there was no real danger. As I came to the end of these thoughts, I realised that I had now been walking for some time and had nearly arrived at the office.

This was the last time that I had such marked symptoms after visiting someone who was ill. It seems that by means of the teaching I had begun to accept illness, and to so great a degree that I had overcome my fear of it.

A few days later I wrote in my diary:

"My problems, as my discipleship progresses – and through this, my therapy – bother me less and less and are milder, but when they recur, I am able to deal with them, since I am learning to resist them less and less. Most of the hours of the day I am completely calm, and I do my jobs with pleasure and without feeling upset. And the most important thing is that I can read, and write my diary for hours, and during these hours I feel very pleased. Difficult problems now seem simpler to me because I have more or less accepted what the Master has told me: 'All these things are a part of life'. I believe that when the 'more or less' goes and I arrive at the point of accepting success and failure, health and illness, as well as all of humanity alike, I shall have been liberated."

SOCIOPHOBIA

It was one of those evenings which I spent curled up and shaking on the sofa of our sitting-room, about a year before my discipleship with the Master began, when the telephone suddenly rang and my husband answered it. I realised from the conversation which took place that it was an invitation to a meal with a family who were friends of ours.

In a moment my heart began to beat faster and harder, I was drenched in cold sweat, and, as always, in these cases, I ended up taking a strong dose of tranquilliser.

After my husband had allowed me to come round a little, he started his attempts to persuade me to accept the invitation. Among the other things he said to me was that we couldn't always turn down invitations, never invite anyone to our house, and, generally, live isolated from everyone. In the end, I promised him that I would accept the invitation.

There was a week between the day of the invitation and the day of the occasion. A week of torment for me. And so, on the day of the visit, when there had been endless thoughts of the type: "You won't be able to carry it off", "You mustn't go, because you'll be made a laughing-stock", "You won't be able to follow their conversation", "It's sure to be torture for you", etc., I was in a very poor state. What made the situation worse was the fact that I couldn't avoid this visit after I'd accepted the invitation. I had promised my friends and my husband that I would try to leave the house for a little.

Whenever in the past we had planned to go out, I was always in a state of panic on the day. In spite of this, I sometimes managed to emerge from this state and keep to our programme. In these cases, however, I was helped by the thought that I could change the plan, even at the last minute.

That day, this was not a possibility for me, and so when we reached our friends' house, the situation was not under control, despite the fact that I had taken a large dose of tranquilliser first. The presence of other people at our friends' house made things worse, so that my stay there – for about an hour – developed into a real martyrdom. It was my husband who got me out of this difficult situation; when he had said that he was sorry to our hosts, explaining that he had to get up very early the next day, he told me we should go.

This failure brought me into greater isolation. My contacts with people began again much later, and only after my discipleship with the Master had gone ahead. From this I learnt that my fear of being in a new environment showed my need for recognition, which led to my anxiety about rejection. It showed that I was afraid of coming into conflict with people, in case I lost the approval of my ego. And, of course, much later I learnt that concealed behind this fear was the need for union, and, first and foremost, the need for union with my partner.

At this point I should not omit to quote what Klairi Lykiardopoulou has written in her book 'The Woman's Role in Contemporary Society': "All needs are one only: the need for union. This union is in essence the love which unites all things. All of us are looking for love, and when we don't find it, we react against this and turn love into hate, fear, hostility, and illness."

The subject of sociophobia was of special interest to me, because I realised that I had suffered from it from a very early age and that it had been handed on to me by my mother, who was constantly tormented by all kinds of phobias, as she was, without knowing it, of course, in total separation from my father. During the course of her life, there was nobody to instruct her in the teaching of union, or even in something simpler: that no one is superior to anybody else, as all are equal before God. The result of this ignorance was that she lived all the time with fears, with retentions, and with worry. And, worst of all, she bequeathed all this to her child.

Sociophobia tortured me a great deal, and put a brake on my professional career and my general progress. I can remember that every time that I was going to take an exam, I had a tendency to vomit, and I shook all over. It is typical that I used to say that if I needed to take only oral exams, I would never manage to pass them, even though I was a good student.

The punishing effects of this phobia are clearly apparent in the incident which I will narrate below, and which, although it was 20 years ago, is still very vivid in my memory.

On one occasion, as treasurer of the union of employees of the department where I worked, I had, at the general assembly of our union, to read out its budget. I remember, as if it were yesterday, how I felt. It was the day when I came to understand the real meaning of the word 'despairing'; this was because the thought of admitting my inability to speak in front of people to my colleagues filled me with shame, just as the thought of agreeing to read out the budget filled me with terror. In the end, my fear overcame the shame, and I admitted to the others what it was that I was afraid of. They were thunderstruck by this confession. They were unable to believe that behind this dynamic trade-unionist a fearful individual was concealing herself. They were discreet enough not to question me. One of them simply stood up and read the budget.

But the problem didn't stop there, just as it didn't end after every incident of this kind. This was because although I used to avoid situations which caused my fear, afterwards I followed yet another wrong practice. I would begin to reproach myself, to tell myself that I'd been wrong, that I ought to find the courage to speak, and, of course, all this caused new guilt feelings and new phobias.

On the subject of sociophobia, the psychoanalysts say that it is a person's fear of appearing before other people, in case he is put to shame. They say that its chief characteristic is a permanent fear of one or more social situations in which the individual is exposed to possible criticism by others.

It may include a fear that he is not able to speak in public, to eat in a public place, or to write in front of others. Exposure of the individual to these situations causes in him acute anxiety and avoidance, even though he realises that his phobias are groundless.

In the case of sociophobia, that is, the individual sees others as judges and himself as being judged, and the result is that he processes information in a catastrophic way. The symptoms of this phobia can lead the sufferer to total social isolation.

One day a girl came to my house to help me to clean. From the very first moment there was something about her which I couldn't accept, and this upset me because up to then I hadn't had a problem with the girls who came to help me from time to time.

The same afternoon, I was seized by an anxiety, which increased as time went on. In the evening I tried to discover what it was that was bothering me. By searching and questioning myself, I found, to begin with, that I hadn't liked the ease with which the girl asked me to make some coffee for her, and then I had been annoyed because, while she was drinking it, she smoked two or three cigarettes. I didn't like the fact that, although the girl was seeing me for the first time, she treated me familiarly and as an equal, without feeling at all that she was in an inferior position.

My egoism couldn't accept this and reacted by saying: "She ordered her coffee as if she'd gone into a café, and began to smoke one cigarette after another". So there it was – another reason for my annoyance. Smoking! I don't get on very well with cigarettes, because my husband smokes a lot. So it was again the same problem which was hiding behind my non-acceptance of the girl.

At my next meeting with the Master, I asked him if the analysis which I had carried out was right.

"Why shouldn't it be right", he replied, "since I've given you the key to enter the castle of truth? And this key, which is also the solution to our problems, is the understanding that there is no such word as 'other', that the other is ourselves. But I will add something to your analysis. You know how man refers to feelings, to impressions.

This is a given, but there is also something deeper. We have, for example, a problem. We discuss it, we work on it, and we decide what we will do, depending on what it is saying inside us. We go deep into our selves, and attempt to avoid first impressions. In this particular case, certainly smoking was a cause.

But there must be others. I believe that what bothered you a lot was this girl's boldness, the ease with which she lays claim to everything in life, as if she is saying: 'Why should I be shy, why should I hesitate to take from life the share that belongs to me? I'm no different from you, I'm not even 'other'. I am an extension of your self. And what I ask for, I'm asking from myself.' And it bothered you because what is lacking from you is this boldness. What you must do is to see whether this person should be with you. If this will be for her good."

I must admit that I wasn't expecting such an answer. I was asking whether I should keep her after her inappropriate behaviour, and whether this would help me, and the answer was that I should see whether this was helping her. I had forgotten that there was no such word as 'her'.

At some point in my diary, a few days after the beginning of my discipleship, I write as follows:

> "I notice that while the company of certain people creates problems for me, because their behaviour fills me with anger and I want to tell them that it isn't right, on the other hand, I don't make up my mind to tell them, and so I let them oppress me. It seems that the fear of rejection predominates in my mind. And, when I'm doing my jobs, instead of thinking of God, of praying, and of glorifying Him, I'm calling to mind all the things which I ought to tell them, but on the other hand I know that I do not yet have the strength which I need to do it. And the more I think of these things and debate about them with myself, the more the psychological conflicts flare up within me, and, together with them, the intensity of my symptoms."

It is clearly apparent from these words that when I wrote them, I was only at the beginning of my discipleship. Apart from anything else, I believed that this behaviour on my part was satisfying some need of theirs. At that time I couldn't make out whether this need was only apparent, and whether a dynamic expression of my views and thoughts on a conscious dissociation from certain mistaken views and positions of theirs would be a real service on my part. But, even if I had known, again I wouldn't have been able to help them, because I would first have had to find the strength which I lacked to recognise, to accept my own negative aspects, and to be delivered from these.

It is obvious that I was trying to project on to those around me a 'mask' that included all these features which I believed would help them to accept me. All my life I have used the energy of my being to build the walls of my personality, within which I hid every time that I should have faced up to something, and I projected outwards only what I believed would win the acceptance of others, which I despairingly sought.

Little by little these walls grew much higher and increasingly prevented the expression of my soul in an outward direction, until I was self-imprisoned within them, within the personality which I myself, without knowledge, had structured. I hadn't understood that those whose acceptance I was seeking were also victims of ignorance of their real self, were projecting their own masks, and were seeking my own acceptance.

An understanding of this erroneous course, anxiety, and inner unhappiness began to come through the teaching. When at some point I wondered whether I was ever myself, the answer which I received from within me was 'no'. What I believed to be my self was no more than a very small part of it, since within every human being is the higher self, which recognises others as its extension and ceases to worry, to fear, to be defensive and aggressive, because nobody fears his own self, nor does he wish to do it harm.

Furthermore, through the teaching, I learnt that each time I am invited to a gathering, so that I am not subjected to anxiety or fear, I should reflect that I am doing this not in order to give pleasure to myself, but because perhaps by my presence I shall be able to meet some need of friends which is probably concealed behind their invitation.

REJECTION AND ACCEPTANCE
OF SLOW RHYTHM

At one of our first meetings, the Master had spoken to
me about singing and its importance as a contribution to
calmness of the soul. Five months later, he returned to
the same subject by asking me:

"What kind of music do you like, Mrs Ioanna?"

"I like every kind of music", I replied, "as long as it
doesn't have a slow rhythm."

"We should like all kinds of music. We should embrace them all. Because when we embrace only one kind,
it is as if we are embracing only one part of our self. But
what is happening to the rest? Even what you have been
suffering from, the whole of your problem, may have its

cause there – in the fact that you don't accept a certain rhythm."

I looked at him in surprise, and a certain amount of disillusionment, because such a conclusion seemed to me peculiar – to say the least.

But, although he realised what I was thinking, he went on serenely:

"Could it be, Mrs Ioanna, that your husband is slow in his movements and that by your failure to accept slow rhythm you are simply not accepting this point in your husband?"

I continued to gape at him with open mouth, not knowing what answer to give, because I was thinking: "Look where we started out from and where we've ended up."

But there my thoughts came to a halt, because the Master continued his analysis:

"You don't accept him at some point. He isn't speedy. But he may not accept your rapidity in decisions, in actions, and so on. He may want it, but he may not be able to unite with it. There are two opposing currents in this field and they must complement one another.

These are currents of the soul which are seeking to be united, but the personalities are reacting against it. In nature there are qualities of inertia, mobility, and harmony. But harmony does not exist if mobility does not achieve union with inertia. It is the complete union of these two which brings harmony. The same thing happens in all the fields."

"And so must I love music with a slow rhythm? But then people who like only classical music are in a state of separation."

"Yes, when something pleases you very much, you should be concerned about this, because there is something concealed behind this preference, as there also is when you dislike something very much. And to come back to you, I tell you that the little which you do not accept is a part of yourself. But you haven't answered my question: is your husband slow in his movements?"

"Yes! It's true that he lives in accordance with a rhythm completely different from mine. He works, of course, long hours, but with a calmness which irritates me. But when he isn't working, he can sit for hours on end with his feet up. If he's watching television or reading, he's equally calm, even if he sees that I'm worried about something – unlike me; I'm not able to calm down, and I worry about everything."

"You have to embrace your husband, to adore him, because he is your male self. Not that you don't love him, or that you hate him, but at some point he doesn't fulfil you completely. You accept him, of course, for the most part because he's your husband, you've had children together, and you also have an attachment to him. But there are some sides of him which bother you. It isn't enough that you should accept him for the most part, and reject him as regards the rest. You must begin to notice each time that you are attacked by your symptoms what it is in your husband that you don't like, everything that annoys you and you don't agree with: every attitude, act, or thought which he expresses, and which, by your resistance to it, makes you ill. Then you will try to discover what lies behind this action which bothers you.

You have to realise that all the problems are created by resistance to union with your husband, and this is due to a fear of the limitation of your individual ego. When you start out from the position that your husband is your male, as you are his female, self, and, therefore, since he is a part of your self, you will see that you can't reject some of his aspects, because this means rejection of some aspects of your own self and will lead to illness. You must look for the cause of everything you don't like in him. This, of course, can't be done from one moment to the next. It needs time. But the more you look, the more you will discover that on the majority of issues the problem is yours."

It is a fact that the whole of this analysis made me do some hard thinking, because I reflected that there are lots of things that I don't like, and if each of these is also connected with some aspect of my husband which I am rejecting, how am I to make sense of it? The Master brought about the conversation about singing and gave me the opportunity to tell him what I didn't like, and for him to explain to me what lies behind this rejection. But how was I to discover all the rest of the things?

And so, I concluded, according to the Master's teaching, in those cases where one of the couple does not accept some opposing fields in the other – and doesn't know this, of course – there is a problem; a problem which may break up their relationship, or lead to mental or physical illness. However, the most important consideration is that non-acceptance will be perpetuated and the couple will never reach complete union of souls, the essence of love. Is it, then, enough for one of the two to learn to work, or must both of them work to bring about some result?

Knowing that the issue of the relationship of the two sexes is not an easy one to manage, and knowing also that it is one of the most important problems which torment mankind, I thought that it would be very useful for everybody to find out what they should look for in the person they are intending to spend the rest of their life with. What characteristics can convince someone that he can live with someone else without having problems? Or what points in him, or how many of these, can one ignore and say: "It doesn't matter. I'll manage to accept these".

The Master's answer to all these questions was as follows: "There's no need to search for those things that you don't accept in your husband. Union with your husband will be consummated if at every moment you function to-wards him through both the mind and heart. The love of God, Mrs Ioanna, is what created the world. And woman is a source of that love. Woman can by her love bring everything into balance, because she is the soul of things."

"But, Master, is it enough for the woman only to work? If she is the only one who works – the other, what does he do?"

"But haven't we said that there isn't 'another'? Haven't we said that we shouldn't think that there is 'another' if we want to emerge from ignorance and see things as they are in reality? A lot depends on the woman. The question is who is this woman and who are you."

"What do you mean?"

"I mean whether you are in essence, in the heart, whether you act with love, whether you are in happiness. If you are waiting for happiness from outside, from your husband, you will never find it. It is only within yourself that it will be found. And if you find it within you, you will be constantly in a state of happiness. Then you adore your husband, your male self, and you accept any aspect of him, since, in any event, it is you who gives birth to these aspects.

The aspects of your husband are as if they are your children. Don't you love your children? What are you waiting for to be happy? For your husband to look after you? Who should look after the other? You must look after him, since you give him rebirth continuously. And only because you take care of him are you happy. You can't blame your husband, because he is yourself. Just as you say that you've made a mistake, you must say the same thing about your husband. There is no happiness outside this understanding. What is important is that you should see in yourself what you are living, what you are experiencing.

If you look for truth in forms, you'll never find it. You will find it in the essence. You have gone no further than the external forms, and you've said: 'What is this Master talking about? This situation here never ends'. If, Mrs Io-anna, you have your husband in your heart, you feel his resting, it flows in you. His legs are your legs. His need is your need. He is you, because he is the half of yourself. You don't feel the half of yourself? But this is death. So you should wake up, and sense the other half of your self. In this way, when you see him sitting with his feet up, you will feel that it is your own feet that are resting.

From the moment that you realise that you must unite with the other half of your nature, you have the key, the basis. Can someone live without his self? Of course not. We should never forget that. When we understand it, we are face to face with ourselves and everything is made one, there is love, wisdom, happiness, greatness. Outside that truth we are in separateness. We see someone, and that person today is good, tomorrow is bad, and so on. For that reason couples who marry because they are madly in love in the end separate. Because such love is only a feeling. It has no relation with the mind, with the essence, with deepening, with the knowledge that we are both man and woman."

"You know, these days I have had more acute upsets, and when I've looked into the matter I've found that recently I have begun to distance myself from my husband again, whereas I'd believed that I'd come closer to him."

"Quite simply, you had reached a compromise. But now you are called upon to take him into a greater embrace. Happiness is cultivated as a flower is cultivated. But in order for it to be cultivated, the union which will develop the seed is required. Man tries to find the things that he is interested in outside him. He seeks to experience them outside himself. But this is a mistake. They are all inside himself, if only he recognises them, and knows that the 'other' is within him. Just imagine that I was wanting something from you because I'm helping you to get well. Wouldn't I be a wretched person? Because I have you in my heart, I have everything."

"For us, Master, it's difficult to reach that point. It requires a lot of work."

"Yes, it requires cultivation and work. But the work is also within our nature. When man doesn't work, he can't be happy. Work should be done as a rite and not out of compulsion, but because it fulfils us."

"You know, I've had my husband's first reaction to the writing of the book."

"That's natural enough. It's as if he's saying to you: 'since you don't practise all these things that you hear and write, why are you writing them?' You must tell him everything. You must tell him how you feel about him and that now you are serving your discipleship in this field. You must be honest with him."

The same evening, following the Master's suggestion, I told my husband that I didn't accept some of his aspects, as, for example, the fact that he spends hours with his feet up, watching television, and I asked his forgiveness for that.

"I know that", he said with a smile. "I've been hearing it for years. Can you perhaps explain to me, now that you're calm, why you don't accept it? Is it a bad thing – to rest my legs a little when I'm not working?"

"Yes, you're right. I've behaved unpardonably. It's simply that my egoism didn't allow me to accept it, because, it seems, unconsciously, I want you to be concerning yourself with me and not watching television and doing crosswords. And again, as the Master has explained to me, this reaction on my part is due to my unconscious desire to be able to sit down as you do and to feel the calm that you do. And I haven't been aware that the more I don't accept your slow rhythm, the more I resist it, the more the finding of calm of the soul becomes an unattainable dream."

At my next meeting with the Master, I told him this:

"Yesterday I had some disturbances again. And yet all these past days I've been trying to see myself in the person of my husband. So why don't I feel completely well?"

The reply was always the same:

"Quite simply because you are not yet fully united with him. There are certain of his aspects which you don't accept."

"But I thought that after certain things we discovered together and discussed, we'd finished with that."

"So then, if you've finished with it, every time you think of your husband, you should be in ecstasy, in a state of happiness. Are you?"

"No, I can't say that I'm in ecstasy just at the thought of him."

"But shouldn't you be? If a woman doesn't experience ecstasy, what does she experience? If you don't experience ecstasy, you are in the passions, and, as you can't stand them, you put them to sleep. But one day they wake up and come out and become disturbances. And I ask you again: are you in a state of happiness just by thinking of your husband? Does he fill you? Does he flood you?"

"I don't think so."

"Why? You must find the 'why', and you must know

that if a person doesn't live happiness, he's not in spirituality, he's dead. How can you agree to be dead?"

"But does experiencing happiness or not experiencing it, being or not being a spiritual person, depend on me?" I asked him breathlessly, because the analysis had arrived at such a point that I felt overwhelmed and hadn't the strength to speak to him.

"Of course it depends upon you. You're a married woman, you have children, you have a man with you who loves you, and you don't live happiness? And you don't pulsate? You're not happy? But then all these illnesses will come back again."

"Are you?" he asked me again, and, as he looked me in the eyes with acceptance, he gave me the impression that in them he saw my soul, all my unconscious thoughts; then, without waiting for a reply, he went on: "The problem is that because it is the nature of woman to give rebirth to the man, to nourish him, to give him life, when she doesn't do this, she's not well. Just think about the matter, it's very important."

"Apart from some things which we have discovered and talked about together, I'm supposed not to have any other problem with my husband", I said to him, but I don't know whether he heard me, because my voice was barely audible. Unconsciously I knew that what the Master was saying was true, but my personality obstinately resisted and all this conflict had worn me out. The Master, however, because he never acted on the basis of emotion, was determined – in spite of the fact that he saw I was exhausted – to complete the analysis, because he judged that the time had come for me to understand the truth. And so he continued:

"But you yourself said what the problem is just now. You used the expression 'I'm supposed not to have any problem', which means, deep down, that you know that you are not completely united with your husband. Of course, you've taken some steps, you've made some efforts. But you must continue to work in order to arrive at the truth. And truth isn't only saying what you think; it's also being what you say. Truth is also knowledge, just as ignorance is a lie. And you are not in truth out of ignorance, that is, because you don't know that you and your husband are one. When you reach the whole, the truth, then you will be able to see everything as a part of the whole and assimilate it in that truth."

"Now that I think about it, in the early years when we knew each other, and in the early years of our marriage, when I thought of my husband, I felt happiness flooding me, and, moreover, I didn't see his faults. Do you think that I was united with him?"

"You were definitely not united with him even then. At that time, you simply had certain desires which he satisfied for you and this satisfaction of the desires helped you not to see his negative sides. It was a convenience for the personality. But as your life went on, since this relationship no longer suited you, the personality declared war on the soul, which sought union with the other half of your nature. Your phobias and insecurities are the results of this war. Because, as we've said before, failure to accept fully your partner, the other half of your nature, the other half of your self, means non-acceptance of your own self. This led you to imbalance of the soul, which showed itself in your phobias and the panic attacks which these caused in you."

"Master, what does 'I am united with my husband and accept all his faults' mean in practical terms? Do I see them, notice them, without them bothering me, because I see them as my own faults, because he is a part of my self? But can you discuss with him something you don't think is right and try to make him understand?"

"When you have advanced to union, that is, when you have reached the point where you and he are no longer two people, but one, then you don't disagree with anything, because you don't see in his actions and his words anything but your own actions and your own words.

You won't believe this, but when a couple has reached complete union, when, that is, each of them has driven out his personal ego and they have created the new expanded ego and the new expanded mind, there are no differing views – but even if there are, these are easily settled."

"If a woman has married a man who from the very first days of the marriage behaves towards her brutally, swears at her, strikes her, and if, theoretically, that woman is a spiritual person, can she set that man right, or will her efforts be a waste of time?"

At this point I thought: "Let's see what answer he will give me. And in this case, again, can the woman have the strength to change such a man? Of course not." However, I hadn't finished thinking this when I heard him saying to me:

"Of course she can. Woman by her nature is destined to give rebirth to the man and bring him up again, as she wishes. The question is whether she tries to achieve this rebirth with the divine gift which God has granted her – love – as her sole weapon. And so, even in this case, the answer is 'yes'. The woman can, if she has matured, if she has advanced to spirituality, change him."

At this point I should not omit to quote Klairi Lykiardopoulou's book 'The Couple's Role in Contemporary Society', in which she writes: "There is something which in the end works in what we might call a magical way when steadiness in the position of giving is not affected by anything, even by the fear of being exploited. This 'something' is the new current of life which little by little penetrates the hardest person.

The love of the one can break down the resistance of the other. It is a matter of resoluteness in the decision which will not be affected either by opposing reactions or by the time that the work lasts."

"Master, after the analysis which you've just carried out for me, a question comes to mind again and again. If, as has been demonstrated, I hadn't accepted my husband as regards certain points in him, and perhaps go on not accepting certain others, without knowing it, and so continue not to be totally united with him, why did I believe that it was impossible for me to live without him?"

"The answer is a simple one. You couldn't live without him because, unconsciously, you knew that he is yourself. You have to understand that in two people who are attached to one another – who are, that is, in a state of attraction and then pass on to repulsion – the time comes when these two currents unite within them, because it isn't possible for them to live without their self."

At this point the conversation with the Master came to an end. A few days later it was Wednesday in Holy Week, and I went with a friend to church to attend the Holy Unction service. On the days before I had been quite well, as I was on that day – until we went into the church. There I found that the service had already begun. Within a fraction of a second I felt my legs give way under me from fear, and at the same time I began to feel dizzy and that I was simultaneously there and not there. I had shut myself into myself again, I had focused my mind on my problem, and a voice was saying to me: "The service won't be over for a long time. You won't make it. You'll have to go, as you've done so many times before."

I summoned up all the forces that had remained in me, sat on a chair, and tried to detach my mind from the single thought on which it was stuck: "It won't be over for a long time".

First I allowed myself to relax, to the extent, of course, that this was possible at that moment, and I tried to 'empty' my mind of every thought. I had taken some time over this effort when suddenly the answer to my earlier thought came into my mind: "So what? What does it matter if the service takes a long time? You'll have time to pray, and to listen to the divinely-inspired words of the Fathers of our Church, which is something you have an absolute need of."

So that was it! I had succeeded in getting my mind to function. Without wasting any time, before the negative thoughts which I had had before returned, I began to look for the reason why I had felt unwell. I didn't take long to arrive again at the conclusion that the cause of my symptoms was the non-acceptance of the slow rhythm, behind which was concealed my non-acceptance of this aspect of my husband, and therefore the non-acceptance of my own self.

As I had these thoughts and made these analyses, I began to come round and to communicate with the place where I was. I devoted myself to the service and managed to attend all of it. By the time I returned home, I was more or less well.

I experienced the results of my non-acceptance of slow rhythm in many places, such as at the hairdresser's. At the beginning of my discipleship, I wrote in my diary:

> *"The hairdresser's is the place which causes me the greatest anxiety, because I'm forced to wait a long time."* At another point I said: *"Today I got as far as the door of the hairdresser's, but at the thought that I would have to wait a long time, I was seized with panic and went away."*

A few months later, when I had discovered that non-acceptance of the slow rhythm of my husband lay behind the sentence 'I have to wait a long time', I wrote:

> *"Today I'm very pleased because I managed to stay at the hairdresser's for quite a long time without panicking, and without needing to leave before I had finished."*

I also felt acute unease and agitation when I visited public services and banks. The first thing I deduced was that this must have been due to the fact that I had to wait in a queue and it took a long time to finish what I had to do.

Later, however, I noticed that I often had the same problem even if I didn't have to wait at all. So I began to observe the problem and I didn't take long to realise that the people who served me worked at a slow rate.

Included in the Society's programme, apart from the self-study groups, is free discussion, which is attended not only by those who don't belong to any group but also by old members. The subjects discussed are chosen by those who take part in the discussion, which in this way take on a good deal of interest.

At one of these discussions, co-ordinated by Mrs Klairi, although on these occasions I'm always calm, since in this way I find an answer to my queries and have added something to my knowledge when I leave, I felt uneasy and slightly dizzy.

When I arrived home, I began to search for the cause of my indisposition. And I discovered the following: in free discussion, the members frequently bring up the same subjects for analysis. It seems that this annoyed me, because I was forced to listen to Mrs Klairi analysing the same subject again and again, and to attend a discussion which unfolded at a 'slow rate'.

Since, because of my egoism I believed that I had learnt everything and was wasting my time listening to the same things over again, whereas Mrs Klairi could have used the time to analyse some issue which I would have brought up for discussion, I didn't accept the situation and so became ill.

My resistance was so great that it didn't allow me to reflect that, a few months earlier, I had gone to the Society in a terrible state, that some people had spent innumerable hours of their time in helping me, that they needed to explain some matters to me endless times before I understood them, without their ever resenting it. I didn't reflect that I too should now convey to others what I had learnt.

Another typical example of non-acceptance of slow rhythm is the following: one evening I went with my husband to a nightclub where a party was being held by an association in the area where we live. I agreed to go only after considerable insistence on the part of my husband, as I was afraid that because of the large number of people who would be there I wouldn't manage to stay for long.

The surroundings were very pleasant, but there was a lot of noise. To begin with, I was slightly uneasy. But when a well-known singer began to sing modern songs to a slow and – in my view – monotonous tune, my condition suddenly worsened. I began to feel dizzy, my heart raced, and I was bathed in cold sweat. I was patient and tried to overcome the problem, but had no success. Things got worse and worse. I was about to tell my husband that we should leave when I saw that the microphone had been taken by another singer who began to sing familiar songs to a cheerful tune.

In a very short time my mood changed. My agitation disappeared and I began to sing. I could have sung all night, but we had to go, because my husband had to work at the office in the morning. When, later, I thought again about the particular incident, I realised that I was continuing not to accept my husband's slow rhythm and that I had to work on that.

I showed a similar reaction one day when my children invited some friends to the house for a meal. I had begun to prepare the food early in the morning. At midday, when I lay down for a little, taking a break from the preparation, I felt a chill at my heart and a pain in my stomach. Analysing this incident, I wrote in my diary:

> *"It seems that, although I have tried, however much I work to put into practice the Master's words that when I am doing a job, I should do it as if I were performing a ritual, that what we are doing must be identified with our inner state and should be done with totality and not under duress, again I haven't succeeded."*

This is what I wrote at the time. But today I see that this was not the only cause. Behind this incident was, basically, my gap, my refusal of slow rhythm, because for the whole process of the dinner a preparation was required which needed time, which was slow to finish. Also, my thoughts were: "Who knows how long they'll sit here? When will they go, so I can get this over with?" But nothing ever finishes. If it wasn't this particular thing which was going on, it would be something else.

Problems never end. As soon as one finishes, a new one comes along, as one cycle of life closes, so that the next can start. Problems come to activate us and to broaden our consciousness and not to restrict us. We should never forget that.

In her book 'The Master' Vol. IV, Klairi Lykiardopoulou gives the Master's analysis on this subject:

"The cycles of life of an individual are endless and are like the cycles carried out by everybody, by the whole of mankind. A cycle is repeated, and so experience is gained, consciousness is broadened, until, one day, that cycle is completed, and then the next one starts. All human beings, and particularly those who are seeking spirituality, project the need to acquire an experience, even if this doesn't always happen consciously. Mistakes, difficulties, and all the problems are parts of the cycles which help in the acquisition of knowledge. For that reason, those who have qualms of conscience and guilt feelings about their mistakes should see themselves at a stage of broadening in each cycle of consciousness and experience, and, generally, in the cycle of life.

We should see the life of each individual as a mega-cycle which is subdivided in all the fields of action into an infinity of lower sub-cycles. When a spiritual person remains constant in this approach – that all the sub-cycles of his life are parts of one ontological megacycle – then he can connect the doings of everyday life with the super ego. To the extent that this happens, difficulties are lessened. Then the cycles are completed more quickly, because they have been recognised as fields of consciousness which refer back to the overall consciousness."

In the same book, she also says the following about this issue:

"Successive cycles, constant trials on all levels of action which take place within the eternal process. Cycles which become pain and restriction – until they are recognised as an expression of the divine which instructs man in assimilation to it – an assimilation which cannot be achieved to the slightest degree if it has not been acknowledged that all the cycles of life, with all the trials and with every new success which they bring, are none other than sub-cycles of the one ontological cycle in which they open and close, begin and are completed, following the eternal processes of the evolution of beings.

This is an eternal progress which by degrees becomes conscious; it becomes action and a position which makes man say: 'I am carrying out my task, the simple, daily task. I am in no hurry, I don't resist, I'm not anxious that it should finish. I am completing an act, in the knowledge that another will follow, another of the endless actions which begin and end every moment in eternity. I am healing the weakness which puts itself forward each time, as well as I can, and I reflect that all men are doing the same, throughout the length and breadth of the earth'."

THE EGO

"Is there anything more beautiful than the union of two souls who have decided to become disciples in the orbit of life? Is there anything more sacred than the embrace of the couple when this is done with the whole heart and is not inhibited by any difficulty?"

This question is put by Klairi Lykiardopoulou in her book 'The Couple's Role in Contemporary Society'. When I read these words, my reply was: "No. Certainly, there is nothing more beautiful". But at the same time I asked: "What is it, then, that prevents this union of souls, and, consequently, the fulfilment of man?"

The answer which the Master had given me, as I have already said, was the following: "Ignorance is the cause of fears, inhibitions, and retentions. And in the case of the couple, this fear has to do with the loss of the individual 'ego'. But the couple do not realise that when this union is achieved, the ego is not merely restricted – it is enlarged."

In spite of the fact that the teaching on the acceptance of my partner and union with him continued, six months after I had met the Master, I wrote in my diary:

> "I have understood this part of the teaching and I have come to believe that this union is the only thing that can cure me. I work constantly and I am advancing along this path, and yet my phobias still make their appearance, at rare intervals, of course, and with less intensity and duration, but they do appear.
>
> There are, moreover, certain things that I have not attempted to do, such as, for example, a long trip. Every time I have such an opportunity, I let it go by, and find some excuse or other. But I know very well that the reason is something else: my fear! And fear comes because union with others or with myself has not yet progressed far enough. And I don't say that this union has not been achieved, that it has

not become an attitude, a way of life, because I
believe that very few human beings experience
this happiness."

Although I had answered my question as to why the phobias continued to visit me on my own, as can be seen from the extract above, at my next meeting with the Master I asked him:

"Why is it, Master, that yesterday, when we went out for a meal with friends, I felt bad, and as a result, didn't enjoy going out?"

"What was it that you thought again, and so let yourself get ill?"

"Quite simply, when we were setting out from home, I was thinking 'what if I don't manage it? what if I have heart trouble?' – and all that sort of thing."

"But don't you understand, then, why all that takes hold of you? Because at that moment you are thinking only about yourself. You are saying: 'I hope nothing goes wrong with me'. It's as if only you exist on the planet. If you don't stop living only for yourself, if you don't begin to be interested in people as a whole and do something for that whole in whatever way you can, even by means of a positive thought, there is no way that you are going to overcome your problem. But, as you will realise, now things have become much easier for you, because now you know the way to emerge each time from separate-

ness, and so to create the conditions for a more substantive union."

The examples I could give to show how much power is
hidden in the personality and how much it resists union
and acceptance are endless. I will quote a few very typical
instances.

One evening, after the end of one of the free discussions which took place at the Society with Mrs Klairi, I
spoke to a lady who is an old member of the Society. She
asked me if I knew the titles of certain books from which
she could find material for an assignment she was going
to undertake. I willingly told her not only the titles, but
that I would give her the books themselves, as well as
any notes I had on them.

It would have been natural for me to be satisfied that
I had been given the opportunity to be of service to the
lady, and, moreover, in something which would help her
to hand on some items of knowledge to other members of
the Society, and for a short while those were my feelings.
However, immediately afterwards I lost this pleasure and
asked myself: "Why? What's happening to me?" I was giv-
en the answer by a voice which came from within me and
said: "Why should you give her the books and the notes?
Why doesn't she go and find them for herself, as you did,
and sit down and read them – as you had to? So have
you tired yourself to find the material, and she's going to
present it?"

When I came to myself and realised what kind of thoughts I'd been having, I said: "How could I possibly be thinking in this way after so much teaching that I have received, after so much help that I have been given, after so much work, after which I'm supposed to have learnt how to serve in an unselfish way?" "And yet, it's possible", I concluded. "And it's possible because there is this beast which is called the 'ego' and which is always wanting something. And in this particular instance, it didn't want to be deprived of the pleasure of hearing some congratulations on its knowledge. But what knowledge? Is this how you acquire knowledge – by reading a book or two? But even if you become a walking library, how will that benefit you if you haven't learnt the truth, if you don't tell the truth, if you are not the truth, and, most important of all, if you don't hand on this knowledge to others? You won't benefit at all, of course. Because this will be yet another example of your great egoism, which, the bigger it is, the more it restricts your life, the more it stifles you, until you fall ill."

Another example of egoism was this: one evening, I went with a group of friends to Rafina for a beer. My husband was enjoying the company and the food, but I complained all the time, and told him that he shouldn't be eating and drinking a lot, because he was getting fat and it wasn't good for his health. Naturally enough, it wasn't long before I was feeling unwell.

When, at my next meeting with the Master, I told him what had happened, believing that I was in the right, because my complaining was intended to protect my husband from possible illness, I was surprised to hear him tell me:

"No, Mrs Ioanna, the real reason for your complaining wasn't that. Unconsciously, you were jealous because he was in a state of happiness which you didn't feel yourself, since you didn't accept yet another side of him – the fact that he is overweight, and so you were in separateness. You should speak to him sincerely again, and ask his forgiveness."

This is what I did. I repeated to my husband the analysis which the Master had made, and I promised that in what he says and does I will see myself. And in order to show that my interest was real, I told him:

"You have to know that if anything happened to you, I shall not be able to bear it, and in a little while I shall follow you."

I expected that my words would move him, but I heard him say to me: "That is to say, again you've thought about yourself". It wasn't even a minute since I was assuring him that I would try to change and wouldn't think only of myself, and yet I was doing the same thing once more.

When, later, I thought over this incident, I discovered yet another reason why I attacked my husband every time that, in my opinion, he ate and drank more than he should. This attack of mine expressed my non-acceptance of the change of the form and my unconscious fear of this change, which leads to old age.

This discovery of mine helped me to explain and to understand why I was resistant to the acceptance of another fact. Recently, every time that my husband got up from his armchair, I told him that he had made its cushion out of shape, and the way he got up, which was different from the way in which he used to, was to blame for that. And every time he would reply that he used to weigh 20 kilos less then, and that, in any case, if the armchair got damaged, we'd buy another. By this reaction on my part I was again expressing an unconscious fear about myself, about old age, and about my death.

Another example of egoism was the following: one morning, when I was going to the office with Dionysis, we called at the garage and left our car to be repaired. We then stopped a taxi to take us to our destination. I had sat down in the back seat when Dionysis opened the front door and I heard the taxi-driver say to him: "Be careful you don't hit the car".

At the same time I also shouted to him: "Be careful, because the car you'll hit is ours!" Then the taxi-driver said to me angrily: "So that's it, is it, madam? You didn't give any thought to my car, with which I earn my living? Are you so selfish?"

I realised at once what I had said and was ashamed of my attitude, but this honest observation of myself and the setting aside of the personality lasted only for a few seconds. The ego made its appearance again, and more powerfully this time, and, instead of begging pardon, I began to find various excuses.

"But, madam", the driver said, even more angry this time, "can you possibly not have realised what you said? All that you cared about was that your car shouldn't be damaged!"

All this conversation had started to annoy me and I was ready to tell him to stop and we would get out. Apart from anything else, I was irritated by the fact that I was being told off by a taxi-driver. Fortunately, Dionysis realised in good time what my intentions were and intervened: "Mother, the problem is not to establish whether by what you said you were thinking only of your own interests; that's for sure. The question is that you should admit the truth and not do it again. Anyway, you haven't committed a crime – that happens with everybody. All of us act in an egoistical way."

The only result which his words produced was that I didn't say a word until we arrived at the office. And so I gave the driver the opportunity to tell me off throughout the journey.

When I was alone and began to think over the scene, I saw that I had acted wrongly. My mistake was not only that I had said something so egoistic, but, above all, that I didn't find the strength to accept the fact in front of others. How many times had the Master talked to me about the importance of honesty! About how important it is that what we say should be what we think. Because, when we don't act in this way, and since others are an extension of ourselves, it is ourselves, in effect, fooling our own selves.

At this point, one of the moral precepts of Athenodorus, the famous teacher of antiquity, came into my mind:

"You should know that you have not yet been freed from your passions if you haven't arrived at the point of not asking God for things which you couldn't ask for in front of other people.

You should live with people as if God is watching you, and speak to God as though people can hear you."

However, the words which were for a long time going round and round in my head were those of a great admirer of Athenodorus, Seneca: "There is a holy spirit within us, the observer and guard of our good and bad thoughts. When you do something good, everyone can find out about it. But when you do something bad, what is the good of no one knowing about it, when you yourself know it?"

One day, after work, we had to go to a notary's office to sign a power of attorney. I had told my husband about this the evening before and I'd also told him that next day he should be suitably dressed.

His answer was that if I wanted him to wear something different from the clothes he usually wore at the office, I should take him some myself. And there the matter rested. The next day, he left home dressed in his everyday clothes, and when I went later, I forgot to take him something more suitable.

When we set out, I had begun to grumble because his shoes were not cleaned and he wasn't wearing a suit or a tie. In other words, he wasn't dressed as I would have wished. For a time I believed that I had accepted the situation, but on the way I took a tissue out of my bag, opened it, and in a harsh way told him to stop the car on the edge of the road and dust his shoes. That was it. He exploded. With angry movements he stopped the car and got out. I'd succeeded in making him angry by clearly demonstrating my rejection. And as if that was not enough, I opened my own door and threw away the tissue, shouting at him:

"You're hopeless. It's a waste of time talking to you. You're not going to change in any way."

When we set out again, I was shaking with anger, and, as always happens in these cases, I didn't utter a word.

He was, as usual, the first to speak to me – calmly, as though nothing had happened: "Tell me, Ioanna, why are you angry with me when you know that you are to blame? It doesn't bother me at all that I'm not wearing a suit – you know that. So, since this is your problem, why didn't you bring me some clothes to change into?"

Instead of taking the opportunity to give a calm reply, to put an end to the matter, I ignored him, and shut myself into myself even more. Soon after, I felt something like a hand squeezing my throat and making it difficult for me to breathe. I turned my head in the seat, and for a long time I was unable to relax or to set my mind to work. When I finally managed to think, I realised at once that I wasn't right, that again the problem was mine and not my husband's, and that I had to solve it on my own, because he was indifferent to the issue of how he was dressed.

He never in his life wore a tie unless I grumbled at him. And so, every time we were to go somewhere, we had a quarrel over this matter. I wasn't applying what the Master says – that we should not invest in the form and in appearance, but in the essence. Thus the cause of my problem was again egoism and non-acceptance, the negative energy which is not converted into love, is not diffused, is not earthed, but remains in the body and produces pain, fear, distress.

Yet again I was seeking the solution to a problem of my own from my husband. Again some 'I want', some desire of mine had created it. And the 'I wants' are endless, just as the problems which they produce are endless.

When I analysed what had happened and accepted that the mistake was mine, I began to feel somewhat better and was quite satisfied. My satisfaction didn't last long. When we were in the notary's office, I heard myself saying: "Please forgive us that my husband is not appropriately dressed, but, you know, we have a building site which he visited a short while ago, and he hasn't had time to change."

So that's the point I had arrived at: I had resorted to lying, in order to satisfy my egoism.

When that night I was lying in bed and thinking over all the events of the day in a calmer frame of mind, I realised yet again how hard the personality fights the soul of man – how much alertness is needed if you are not to be led astray by your egoism. Because while you think that you've managed it, you very soon realise that the opposite is true: that again you have been shut into your egoism.

Therefore, again you are ill. I discovered that every time that what I wanted didn't happen, as in the present instance, I rebelled and my soul was flooded with anger. But what did I gain by that? I was the one who suffered and was unable to be at peace, but, more important, I made those around me suffer and get angry. And that is not the only unpleasant aspect of the matter, because scientists have proved, as a result of research, that anger is destructive for human beings.

Dr Segal, professor at Stanford University, reported to a conference of the Society for Nuclear Medicine that anger is a major danger for heart patients, because it significantly reduces the quantity of blood pumped by the heart. Dr Williams of Duke University, a specialist researcher in behavioural matters at the University's Medical Centre, noted: "Anger kills". Researchers, in general, have demonstrated that quarrelling seriously damages the health.

The writer Athanasios Landos, who lived in the sixteenth century in Crete, in his book entitled 'The Salvation of Sinners', writes as follows:

"Anger which is not controlled by the reason conceals a tendency towards revenge and has as a consequence that the individual is distressed needlessly, or more than he should be. What you must try to do is not to be dominated by anger and not to let it take precedence over reason; because anger is followed by rage, quarrelling, fighting, insults, and the rest.

"What we must do is to strive truly not to be overcome by anger. Here it is helpful to distance yourself for a little while from the person with whom you are angry and to involve yourself in some work, until the flame of your anger dies down, so that your mind can play a part in your decisions. We all know that when we are angry we say and do things which afterwards we regret. And, furthermore, we all know that when our anger has passed and we have calmed down and realised that we were wrong, our egoism does not permit us to ask forgiveness and to admit our fault." And he concludes: "The disturbance of anger sinks the vessel of Discernment of the mind".

About anger and its consequences – the sinking of the mind in the emotions – the Master had told me the following:

"One of the seven energy centres of man's body is the solar plexus. This centre is in the abdominal area. This is where all the emotions have their seat and it is from here that they emerge as energy into space. Its chief characteristic is fulfilling an emotional desire. It is through this centre that, in terms of consciousness, the human individual ego developed in the course of the evolution of mankind. When, therefore, there is anger or any other emotion in man, the energy descends to the solar plexus, charging it, and, in this way, the quantity of energy in the brain is reduced, so that the mind does not play a part in the decisions, the actions, the words which man uses to deal with the situation."

As to anger, my thinking was that every time I get angry, I forget the teaching of St Paul: "love does not behave in an unseemly fashion". Love does not express itself in a unseemly way. But today, just as on innumerable other occasions, I had expressed myself in an unseemly way, and in the end had told my husband: "I'm wasting my breath, there's no way that you are going to change". So there was the prejudice!

The conviction that it wasn't possible for any change to take place. My prejudice viewed the firmness of the other in his convictions as an immovable obstinacy. But how will I know when my partner is expressing his views and his convictions, and not an immovable obstinacy? This, of course, needs time for you to be able to distinguish. But even if, in this particular instance, it was a case of immovable obstinacy in his view about dress, is it possible for his behaviour to change in this way? Is it ever possible with rages, angry outbursts, rejection, without generosity, tolerance, patience – that is, without love – to bring about results?

The practical conclusion which I drew from this particular incident was that if I kept calm, I would be in a position to think and to overcome the problem. In this way I could have avoided the crisis which I had been through. And then I thought: "What would happen if my husband was like me? If he was not calm, patient, without explosions of anger, shouting and quarrelling? If he didn't forget wrongs in a single moment, and didn't forgive me for everything at once? If, in a few words, he didn't have a heart full of true love? In this case, our marriage certainly wouldn't have survived."

It is a consolation that now I am able to see and understand my mistake; I am able to discern what is concealed behind the happening which annoys me, which means that I have begun to cut down on my egoism and to take the first steps towards acceptance and union.

I will conclude this chapter with an extract from what the Master says about the 'ego' in analysing the story entitled 'Guilt' by Dimitris Karvounis in his book 'The Wisdom of the Narrative': "Trapped in his individuality, man, unable, to envision the divine progress, uses himself up in the dimensions of his fictitious ego. He draws himself up to the full height of his egoism, becomes gigantic in his self-centredness, and, oppressing his fellow-men, swaggers because of fear and insecurity. He represents himself as invulnerable and powerful, acts the part of a person of importance, and is capable, on the slightest provocation, of proving his superiority by demolishing everything, without, in most cases, making an apology for the consequences."

THE BENEFICIAL EFFECTS
OF SERVICE

The subject which the Master never ceased to talk about throughout my discipleship with him was service. "Service", he used to say to me, "which is performed in various ways is the realisation in practice of our teaching and forms an important stage in the evolution of disciples. By service is not meant only the donation of material goods.

The meeting of any real need of our fellow-men is service. This may be the meeting of their need to express some problem which they have, and our solidarity, without identification, in this, our psychological support of them, and so on.

In the case of psychological support, caution is need-ed, because service should respond to the deeper need of the human being for balance of the soul. And so we should, every time, discover the real need of the other person, to the extent that we can manage this, and not satisfy merely some apparent need. At all times, of course, there is the possibility of error. But the possibility of er-ror should not, however, lead us to refuse service."

In the early days, every time that he spoke of this sub-ject, I became irritated and replied that throughout my life I had helped and served people as far as I was able. There was, therefore, no reason for us to waste our time on my learning to do something which, in any event, I was doing already. A considerable length of time went by before I realised that he had his reasons for dwelling on the subject. What he was trying to make me under-stand was that the service which I was performing was not conscious, pure service. On the outside, this is what it seemed to be. But unconsciously I was not doing what I was doing only out of love, because, deep down, I was seeking recognition in order to satisfy my egoism. And whilst I believed that I loved people, that I suffered with them, I had to understand that all this was no more than the shop-window of my ego, it was a purely emotional approach, and that my mind and my heart played a very small part in these things, and so what I did seemed to me heavy and burdensome.

Another point to which the Master had drawn my attention from the beginning in connection with service was the control of our own emotions when we are trying to give psychological support to certain people, because we convey our emotions to them as well. If these are positive, our help to them is great, because not only will we pass these on to them, we shall also assimilate their own negative emotions. If, however, they are negative, instead of helping them, we shall have done them harm, because to their already sorry psychological state we shall have added our own.

The Master used to say: "Of course, the offering of positive emotions is a beginning, which usually brings about unstable results, because of their double nature. As the years go by, and if you work on it, you will learn to provide a more substantive form of service, which is that containing the features of the intellectual mind and of love, indissolubly bound up with one another. This service brings about stable results, because in this way we are also helping the other person to pass over his emotional identification and to understand for himself the solution to his problem. But until this happens, service from this position helps us not to become entrapped in the troubled emotional world of the person we are dealing with."

On the subject of the emotions, the psychologist Carl Jung says that these are infectious, and studies of the interaction of the psychological state of individuals have described the emotions as viruses which are passed on from person to person. Just as there are people who are vulnerable to viruses, this is what happens here. That is, the soul too has its immune system, the difference being that man is called upon to safeguard this system on his own by working constantly to reduce his egoism and for his union with everybody and everything, because the complete immunity of the soul is achieved only by this total union.

Scientists speak of the responsibility which we have when we do nothing to change our mood and are at the mercy of anxiety, fears, and all the other negative feelings. In these cases, apart from the fact that we suffer ill effects ourselves, we transfer these feelings on to others. In this way, the dimensions taken on in society as a whole by our bad moods, our melancholy, our complaining, and the whole range of negative emotions is enormous.

I had made discoveries myself about how much our emotions influence others. I had noticed that the influence on me from my visits to sick people was different in each case. I knew, of course, that the agitation which seized me was not only a result of the sorrow which I felt, but above all of my fear of my own possible illness. However, this agitation was not always the same. As a result of my observations, I arrived at the conclusion that

I was being influenced by the psychological state of the patients. When these had accepted their problem and were coping with it calmly, they didn't aggravate my own state. But when they were possessed by fear of their illness, then things became very bad for me, because their feeling of fear was added to my own. And, of course, in the same way I was influencing them.

This influence began to diminish with time, after the work which I did so that I would stop being afraid of illness. In this I was helped by the words of the Master – that illness, like all the negative features of life, is a part of it, and that, in any event, when we have already fallen ill, we can't avoid the problem, but we can help to overcome it more quickly. Thus we shall avoid another possible illness which we can cause by our phobia.

I used to call to mind these words every day. But this was no more than a practical exercise which remained on the surface of things, and, naturally, the improvement in combating my phobias was similar. The real help came with time through the teaching, and through the work which I did on service and union with my partner. It seems that the most difficult thing, but also the most essential, of all, however little we understand this, is to achieve this acceptance and union with the other half of our self, with the other half of our nature. When this happens, acceptance of everything is easier, not to say assured.

A year after the beginning of my discipleship, my phobia about illness had been greatly reduced, without my being able to say that it had been eliminated altogether, which was, anyway, true of all my phobias. But this didn't worry me, because I now knew that, quite simply, I had not accepted my partner totally and that when this happened, absolute calm within myself would come, and – why not? – happiness also.

Before concluding this chapter, I shall give a few examples of service, in order to show by means of these how service, union, the reduction of the ego operate in dealing with our own problems, and in the finding of our own balance of the soul.

One example is the following: it was at the beginning of my discipleship, and one morning I got out of bed not all that optimistic, perhaps because the night before I had felt more unwell than usual. In spite of this, I dressed, and went to see an elderly lady. The day before, her daughter, who lived opposite us, had told me that her mother was in a very poor psychological state: she was afraid she was going to die, and cried continuously.

I hadn't seen this lady since the year before, because she only came to Athens for two months in the winter. The rest of the time she lived in her village. As soon as she saw me, she began to cry and to tell me that she wasn't well and was going to die. To start with, I felt dizzy and was bathed in cold sweat. My heart was beating so hard that I thought it would burst. For a moment I thought that I wouldn't be able to control the situation, but I immediately managed to see it as something which was a given fact. I set my mind to work and to reflect that at that moment a human being needed my help, and this help was nothing other than listening to that person and saying one or two words of comfort.

The first thing I did was to take her for a walk in the very beautiful garden of their house. The sun was shining and this made both of us feel better. I think that when I went away, after an hour, I left her, if not very much, at least a little better. I reminded her that I too had the same problem, that now I was trying by love and with the help of God to overcome it, and that she should do the same.

When I returned home, I was calm; I had forgotten my own issues and was glad because I had managed by my company and the conversation to make this lady feel, if only a little, better, and to ask me, whenever I had time, to go for a chat. This was the first time I realised that service helps you to overcome your own problems. Within us there is an inestimable treasure – love. When we give this treasure to others, we receive our reward at once.

The following is a second example: one morning I visited a friend of mine who was getting ready to have an operation. We talked a little about her problem, we touched on a thousand and one other topics, and I managed to stay with her for more than an hour. When I got home, I realised that all the time the visit had lasted, I hadn't thought of myself, but only of her, and how I could support her by the conversation in her own problem. For the first time, I embraced a health problem with love, without thinking about any possible illness of mine. For the first time I consciously let my soul stretch out and embrace the other person, and for that reason I too felt well.

However, in the early days, I rarely performed this kind of service – through the heart and with knowledge and not with the emotions. And though one moment, by a simple, conscious act of service I felt myself liberated, the next I became again a slave of my egoism. And so, the next afternoon, when I was waiting for this same friend for us to have a chat, I noticed that I had begun to be overcome with unease, which, when she arrived, developed into agitation, dizziness, and the familiar constriction of the heart. I tried to relax, to set my mind to work, to accept all this that was happening to me, but sometimes I succeeded in this, and sometimes not. My fear of illness had surfaced again.

During her visit, we talked about various things – other than our health problems. She told me only that she was going into hospital the day after the next. The positive thing was I managed not to tell her that I didn't feel well. And this was positive because in order to control myself, I did some thinking along the lines of: "How am I going to talk to my friend about the anxiety I feel when she is facing this problem of hers with real calm and composure, just as she did before with more serious health problems? For all this to pass off, I must concentrate, as I did the last time, with real love on her problem, without thinking of myself." These thoughts showed that I had begun to think of others, and not only of myself.

As my discipleship and my efforts to put it into practice progressed, both my decision on conscious service and, together with it, my health had begun to stabilise.

FIRE

In this chapter I shall quote, without adding or removing anything, what I wrote in my diary from 17-7-95 to 20-7-95. I believe that if I change anything, I shall not convey what I really experienced, or the way in which I dealt with it.

17-7-95. For some days now I've not been feeling too well. Today I got up at six in the morning because an operation on my gums was scheduled for the day. From the time that I got up I had tachycardia and agitation, as on the previous days, and this was due to my fear of visiting the dentist – and this is connected to my more general fear of illness, which I haven't completely overcome.

When the doctor injected the anaesthetic, things got worse. I didn't think of asking him if I could leave, and so he went on with the operation, which lasted about an hour.

I wasn't in a very good state when I arrived at the office. It was some months since I had felt like this. Although the dentist explained to me that the injection he had given me often brings about a certain degree of tachycardia, I know that it had affected me very little, because in the past I have had many such injections.

I know that my feeling unwell was due, on the one hand, to fear of illness and, on the other, to something else: to my resistance to the state of affairs which prevails at our house because of the work that has been carried out there for two months now. Of course, in spite of this resistance, I manage to deal with workmen and to attend to more than ten individuals a day. I can stand all the upheaval that is caused, which is something that just a few months ago I could only dream of doing.

When I returned to the office, I drank some milk and got ready to lie down on a couch, to relax

and to calm down. I didn't have time to, however, because the telephone rang and our children told us that a major fire had broken out on
Eastern Penteli and was heading to the area
where we live.

That was all I needed! I became a wreck. Every ten minutes I telephoned the children and
begged them to leave the house and come down
to Athens. I didn't succeed in persuading them,
just as they didn't succeed in persuading me
not to ring them again, because they were helping to fight the fire, which was burning on the
borders of the district. Fear, after such a long
time, had paralysed me and had put my mind
out of action. In the afternoon, my husband told
me to get ready so we could set out for home.
I screamed at him in reply that I wasn't going
anywhere, because it said on television that the
area was on fire.

"That's all very well, but haven't you thought
that our children are there and need our help?
If you don't want to come, I'll go on my own",
he said.

"No! I can't bear that. By the time you get back,
I shall be dead."

"Get up, then, and let's go home."

As I had no choice, I got up from the couch and

tried to stand on my feet. I believed that as soon as I saw the fire, my end would come. With the help of my husband, I managed to get into the car and slump into the seat. I put one hand in the region of my heart to stop it escaping, while with the other I attempted to wipe the sweat from my face. When, after I little while, I tried to speak, I found that I had no voice.

We arrived at the house after a lot of trouble because the police were not allowing traffic in. Throughout the journey, after Stavros at Aghia Paraskevi, we could see the fire and hear the sirens of the fire-engines and the ambulances shrieking. I wanted to shriek myself, but I wasn't able to do so because I still had no voice. But what dealt me the death blow was the spectacle which met my eyes when we turned from Marathonas Avenue towards our house. The fire appeared vast, and the impression it gave me was that it was burning just next to me. When we arrived, I saw that this wasn't the case, that the fire was burning on the borders of the district, but my mind was now more or less out of action.

When I entered the house, I collapsed on to a bed, closed my eyes, and attempted to relax. In a little while I leapt up, because my state, instead of getting better, had got worse. I tried to do all the exercises that I had learnt. The help I got from these was small, but it helped me to think as follows: "Wait a moment, what am I trying to do? Ever since this morning I have been resisting my symptoms and the fire, even though I know that this resistance makes things worse. If I go on like this, I shall end up in my previous state, and this time things will be more difficult. I must accept what is happening and see what to do to get over it as well as I can."

When I concluded my thoughts, I found myself at the kitchen sink, and attempted to do some washing-up. My arms and legs continued to shake, and my heart to beat hard and fast, since I was still in a state of great anxiety. Thus I was not able to concentrate on the work I was doing. However, I had begun to think, and was attempting to do something creative. When I finished, I took a bath, and, when I discovered that the fire was of small extent and that it was moving away from our area, I lay down. Now things were somewhat better. I relaxed and to a certain degree managed to accept the situation, after I had thought over again all the relevant analyses which the Master had made for me. It seems that at some point I fell asleep.

18-7-95. The ringing of the doorbell at two in the morning roused me out of bed in alarm. Neighbours warned us that the fire had flared up again and was approaching us menacingly. At the same time, our children, who had been keeping watch on the top floor, came and told us the same thing. We had to leave our house immediately.

Without knowing how, I found myself standing with a bottle of water and a damp towel outside the car, looking around me. The flames were spreading at lightning speed because of the strong wind. Their tongues were meeting above the houses, which you would have thought were disappearing in them and in the thick smoke. In the end, we got into the car and set out for our office, where we arrived at four in the morning.

Tonight, I have again experienced panic for a little: that state which I can't even describe. All day I have been feeling dreadful, in spite of the fact that we were told that, apart from the garden being burnt, our house had not been damaged. At some point, Mrs Klairi telephoned me. We didn't speak for more than a minute, but this was enough to convey to me her calm, her positive thoughts, and for me to feel better.

On the other hand, all the phone calls which I received from friends and relatives made my state worse, because their negative thoughts and anxiety were added to my own.

Late in the afternoon, I realised that if I didn't want the state I was in to become permanent, I would have to accept the problem again and work to correct whatever I could. That's why I asked my husband if we could go back home.

When we got there, a new blow awaited me. As far as my eye could see, I was looking at nothing but trees turned to charcoal and still smoking. Tears began to flow from my eyes, while my body was shaken by sobs. I entered the house in tears. Everything was covered with ash. My legs no longer supported me. Exhausted, I lay down on a sofa. I felt my powers leaving me, whilst one thought went round and round in my mind: "Now you've gone back again to where you were when you went to the Master. You are in the same mess!"

But immediately another thought came to drive out the first: "But what's this that you're saying? Don't you understand that it's natural for you to feel this way after such a big natural disaster? Don't give in to despair. Get up and try to help your family, who are having the same trying time as yourself. Don't think only of your-self!"

In order not to give myself time to return to the earlier negative thoughts, I got up and began to help my children in tidying up the house. In a little while I realised that I hadn't done any-thing, but was just wandering around in it, and I thought: "Come on now! You've taken the first step, try to concentrate on the job now, because your family needs your help." By pushing my-self, I managed to do a few things. This helped me to distract my mind from the problem and to feel better. The first step, which is also the most difficult, had been taken. From this point on, things were easier. I did the relaxation exer-cises and managed to sleep for a bit.

19-7-95. Today I am better. My symptoms both-er me, but to a lesser extent, and I believe that I shall succeed in becoming as well as I was before the fire.

Yet again, through this terrible experience, I made the same observations as I had recently. The first is that resistance to a situation which I don't like and non-acceptance of it are making me ill.

The second is that the more I think about myself,

and the more I am concerned with illness and its symptoms, the more these things run riot. On the other hand, my participation in events, dealing with unwelcome facts, and the thought that many people are facing the same problem – and in the present case, my own family – make me feel stronger. So here's the medicine: recognition of the needs of others, and the most service possible to them to meet those needs.

My third observation was that on all these difficult days I have been greatly helped through writing my diary. What I am living through, what I feel, the observations and analyses that I make pour out like a torrent on to the paper. And when I finish writing, I feel relief, as if it wasn't me who has been through what I write. My last and greatest observation, however, is that I have learnt to overcome difficulties by the acceptance of the negative aspects of life, of people, of my partner, and so of my own self. A proof of this realisation is the fact that just two days after the great trial we have been through, I have recovered the previous rhythm of life.

20-7-95. Today I began to re-read all the teaching I have received. I can't concentrate very much on reading, but the little that I manage

*does me a lot of good. I try desperately, in look-
ing at all this destruction of nature, to assimilate it into the concept of the good, into the concept of divine love, into the concept that nothing
happens by chance, but everything happens in
order that we should learn something. But from
this destruction, what ought we to learn?*

*Could it be that we should see that earthly
goods do not belong to us and get used to the
idea that we are simply managers of them, and
that we should not have an attachment to them,
because then God may take the management
away from us, because in a single moment everything we have created during a lifetime can
be destroyed?*

*Could it be, again, that we should learn that
man is weak in the face of situations of this
kind? However, he usually lights fires himself,
for some personal benefit. But what is the benefit, when without woodlands, he can't survive?
Is it that he doesn't know that and has to be
severely chastened in order to understand it?*

*And so he is given an opportunity through these
trials to leave behind his complacency and to be
forced to find the divine power which the inner
mind conceals and to emerge victorious, becoming aware of what the Master says in his analy-*

sis of the poem 'Ocean Navigation' by Christos Koulouris in his book 'The Wisdom of the Poem': "Man is not alone; every difficulty is shared by his other self, the holy one, the one that rises up from the matins of the depths. This is the other, the inner experience, that to which man must refer. With the holiness which characterises it, it draws together all his efforts and hopes, it is at his side in his sorrows, it weeps for his misadventures, and directs the fate of all things."

But, even if man does not realise this in his every trial, his own self is not slow to remind him of it.

Only a few days have passed since the great destruction, and today, as I look closely at the blackened trees and the creepers in the garden, I can't believe my eyes. They have begun, beneath the burnt leaves, to put out new shoots. When Dionysis was watering them and telling me that they would turn green again, I replied that nothing springs up from the ashes. But it seems that many things can be born from the ashes. What is important is that we should see beneath these failures and disasters. Do we see only what appears, or do we see eternal creation, God? Do we see only the burnt branches of the trees, or do we see their sturdy

*root, which will make them burgeon and be-
come stronger than they were before?*

Klairi Lykiardopoulou, in her book 'The Master' Vol.
III, provides a more profound analysis of the issue and
gives her own answers to the question of why man fears
the flames which burn the woodlands, houses, and cit-
ies, and to that of why he starts these fires. She writes:
"Fear of flames has to exist, because it is the duty of
every being to protect the form. But man fears not only
fire, but has a similar fear of the fiery power of the spirit.
He resists this, because he realises that for him it will
burn away aspects of some other kind which relate to his
needs, his desires, and his attachments. In this way he
is restricted to these small fires and is not diffused into
the boundless unquenchable fire of the universe which
penetrates him.

The efforts of man to remain shut in his shell are in
vain. The power which overwhelms him does its work
steadily and firmly, and sometimes conquers him, liber-
ates him.

The meaning of the word 'combustion', in relation to
inner processes, refers to the transubstantiation of the
'mini-powers' which make up the entity of man: his instincts, senses, and thoughts. All these things are necessary characteristics of human existence, because
through these it lives, exists, is preserved, and perpetu-

ates its kind. However, besides these needs there is also the spiritual power which in order to be discovered, needs the lesser powers to be dominated and their fires to be assimilated by the non-material flame of the spirit.

More specifically, the power of the instinct must bring about a knowledge of essential union with life, with the other sex, and with the needs of the body more generally. The emotions must be allayed and become only a pure spiritual love for everybody and everything.

The thoughts must themselves be transformed into ideas which bring a direct result, a realisation. In its essence, no single one of the characteristics of man is eliminated, but as it is checked against others which are more expanded, it is directed by them, is transubstantiated, and so a wider consciousness is produced which is the result of the union of the different levels of consciousness.

Arsonists have been flooded by their weaknesses, such as, for example, hatred for the political system of the country or the conditions of life, or simply for themselves. This hatred burns them up and they seek to relieve the tension; they cannot stand the strength of their hate and do not know how to transform it into love, because they do not see the spiritual fire within themselves. Until, in the end, the need for relief overwhelms them and they take out their feelings on the woodlands, destroying everything that is green in entire regions.

They burn, that is to say, a natural form because they do not wish, or do not know how, to burn their negative attitude. As members of the human race, they become channels for human weaknesses and manifest these by their actions. Every arsonist, but also every person who resorts to an intense relief of the feelings by committing some crime or succumbing to his passions, is none other than a negative aspect of the whole of mankind, which, by gaining access to the weaknesses of one individual, is projected through these.

The conclusion drawn from these thoughts is that in different ways all of us human beings do the same thing all the time. We don't check fear against fearlessness; we don't unite the small fires of egoism, of anger, of doubt with their opposites. And so all these things seethe within us, they overheat and break out, causing destruction. Perhaps we don't set fire to trees, of course, but we break up our relationships, we come into conflict with others, we wound our loved ones. In other words, we destroy the beauty of life – and of ourselves – because we refuse to emerge from the constricting features of our nature."

THE DEPARTURE
OF THE MASTER

One afternoon, in October 1994, I was seated in the Society's sitting-room with my eyes fixed on the door of the entrance, waiting impatiently to see the Master come in. It was past the time when he usually arrived and I had started to be worried, because in ten months since I started my discipleship he had never failed to turn up, or was even late. This, of course, is nothing compared to the fact that for many years the Master had never been absent from the Society for a single day.

Every day, even on Sundays and holidays, he was there to give his services to anybody who asked for them, because selfless help for others was for him his sole aim, his life's work, it was his life itself. There was nothing for him apart from the unshakeable position that by caring for others you are caring for an aspect of your own higher self, that is, the entity. I shall never forget what he said to me on the day when he was explaining the subject of service:

"Can you imagine me, Mrs Ioanna, asking for something from you because I am helping you? Wouldn't I be an unfortunate person? But because I have you in my heart by caring for you, I don't want anything."

As I continued to look at the door, I imagined him entering the Society, greeting us with a smile, and beginning his laborious efforts to climb the stairs which lead to the first floor. After the road accident which he had had ten years earlier, this climb must have been a daily martyrdom for him. I believe that nobody else would have consented to be subjected to it in order to put himself at the service of others.

This picture counted within me for as much as thousands of analyses on service and helping mankind. What need did I have of analyses when I had a living example of sacrifice before me? When I was receiving help from someone who would talk with me for hours on end, sometimes sitting in an armchair with his legs, which he couldn't bend, stretched out on a stool, and sometimes half-lying on a sofa, when the unbearable pain forced him to abandon the armchair?

Time passed and the Master did not appear. A worry had started to seize me. I was faced by a specific problem that day and I wanted without fail to discuss it with him. Whom was I to discuss it with if he didn't come? Who would help me? As usual, my thinking revolved around myself. I didn't for a moment reflect that, for him not to come, something serious was happening to him. A fear had started to possess me. It was that very same fear that I felt every time my thoughts didn't go beyond myself.

At some point, a woman disciple told us that the Master would not be coming that afternoon because he was going for some medical examinations. I don't know how long I remained sitting in my place without any communication with those around me. I had the feeling that suddenly I was lost. It seems that Dionysis must have repeated to me many times that we should leave, because I heard him saying to me:

"Oh, come on now, what's got into you? Can't you hear me?"

I got up from my place and followed him to the car. When we were halfway home, I was still in the same state. Dionysis was talking to me all the time – but in vain; I didn't hear a word. The only thing I could think of was: "Whom am I going to talk to about what is on my mind? And if the Master doesn't come back, who is going to help me to deal with my problems?" "You are!" I heard a voice say within myself. "Now that you've been taught the way. The only thing that's necessary is for you to believe in your ability to supply the solutions to your problems and to apply in practice all that you know. The Master has told you many times that nothing is by chance and that we must use every difficulty which presents itself to learn something, and, in the present case, what you must learn is how to rely on yourself and not on others."

The voice of Dionysis, asking me if I was feeling well, brought me back to reality. I didn't stay there long, however, because my thoughts went back two months, to a meeting I had with the Master. That evening, before I wished him good night, he said to me:

"I think, Mrs Ioanna, that it isn't necessary for me to see you so often now. From now on, we'll have a talk only once a week." At that moment, I thought I'd received a hard slap in the face. "But how is it possible", I thought, "that he has suddenly lost interest in me? In the early days it had been he who pressed me for us to meet more often, and I complained, telling Dionysis that this was tiring me, and instead of helping me, was making me worse. Now that I feel the need to see him – every day, if possible – he tells me that I'm to see him only once a week. What's come over him? What have I done to him?" Without externalising my thoughts, I said good night in a barely audible voice and went out of the room.

These thoughts tormented me for days, and so at our

next meeting I told him of them. He looked at me benevolently, and, smiling that gentle smile of his, asked me:

"Do you really believe that things are as you say?"

"It's a fact that after my first impression, I thought that I'd perhaps made some mistake."

"Of course you're making a mistake. It's true that it's not easy for the work of the Master, which is the bringing to the surface of the consciousness, to be understood by the disciple. Deep down, every human being seeks maturity. But there is also immaturity, which wants always to take, to be protected. This immaturity constantly collides with the need for maturity, and because it is precisely maturity which every Master teaches, major internal tensions are created.

The Master teaches autonomy everywhere. And this is the disciple's problem. Because he is afraid of being autonomous, he seeks in the Master the substitute for what he lacks. He wants the Master to behave like a father. And the Master, who knows this, does so to begin with, but little by little he tries to get the disciple to realise that a spiritual relation must develop between them. The disciple must learn to find fulfilment within himself and not in the person of someone else.

The Master is consciousness and knowledge. But he is also ignorance and error. All things teach us; all things are our fathers and teachers. What does 'Master' mean? Anything at all! Do not personify the Master in one person, and do not become attached to him, because in this way you will make no progress.

The Master is all things. And what is expressed consciously by a person, but also what passes unconsciously within us. The Master is the whole of life. Do not deify the Master. The only thing he can do is to show the road, to expand the consciousness, to speak of God. All other ideas that people have about Masters are their own projections; they are not true. A Master is the consciousness in man, but until this is discovered, some guidance is needed, and this is given by the Master."

"Why, to begin with, didn't I come willingly to our meetings, particularly when you asked me to make these more frequent?"

"This happens with all disciples. They believe that there is a problem as regards some specific Master. But no such problem exists. Disciples see it that way because they don't want to see the truth. The problem has to do with their consciousness, with the inner Master. They resist him and project their reaction, which takes on a form with regard to some person. In time, as the concept of inner consciousness develops and is put into practice, the relations of the disciples with the Master become different."

"I understand all this that you're telling me, but I don't think that I can apply it in practice, at least now. For the present, I think I have a need to see the Master personified in you. However, by all this analysis you have convinced me that the reduction in the number of our meetings is not because your interest in me has become less, but, on the contrary, it is for my good. It seems that you have detected some attachment to your person on my part."

"Yes, there is that too. But it isn't only that. I have seen that you can now be taught by the inner Master."

"You know, by all this analysis you have made for me, you have also answered another question, something which has concerned me since the beginning, when I met you, and which I haven't dared to put to you. This is: why, when you teach, do you always use the third person and not the first? The first time I heard you say 'The Master says', my mind went to some mysterious Master, superior in rank to you, who doesn't condescend to come into contact with the disciples. Also, that he forbids you to convey his teaching to the disciples as your own, and so compels you to use the third person. All these thoughts created ugly emotions in me. But these became different after Dionysis assured me that there is no other Master. However, it's only now, after all you've told me about the inner Master, that my questioning has been answered, because I've realised that he is the one you are referring to, he is the one who 'says'."

As I thought about all this, the car stopped outside our house and I, before I got out, had a last thought, which filled me with optimism: "Today, for the first time, the inner Master functioned within me."

My discipleship with the Master came to an end effectively on 7 December 1994. After that date he didn't come to the Society again. The illness from which he was suffering forced him to go in and out of hospital, and to stay at home. Of course, my contact with him hadn't stopped, nor had it with all the disciples, since even at the time when he was ill, he thought only of us.

He knew that some of us had a relation of dependence with him, but he was certain that – as proved to be the case after the event – after the teaching we had received, this form of relation would dissolve and would give place to the correct Master/disciple relation, to the spiritual relation to which the emergence through us of the inner Master, in the sense of consciousness, life, of the spirit, would lead us.

The first time I visited him in hospital, I felt very disturbed. That day, the patient I would be seeing was not a relative or friend, but the one who supported me every time that my fear of illness and death surfaced. I went into his room pressing myself very hard, and I was prepared, as far as I was able to manage this, to be faced with a seriously ill person, but my surprise will be understandable when I saw the same smiling, calm face which I knew, and heard the same strong and warm voice greeting me. He gave me the impression that he was sitting in his armchair at the Society, and not lying in a clinic bed after the very serious operation on the ileum which he had undergone. My worry at once began to lessen. When I left, after the hour's teaching I received, not only as a result of what he said to me, but, above all, because of what I had seen, I was perfectly calm.

Contact between us continued, sometimes by telephone, and sometimes by my visits to the clinics, for about a year, and each time he never missed the opportunity of stressing to me that now, and for my further spiritual progress, his presence was not necessary. By these words he was hinting that he would soon be leaving us.

On 21 December 1995, the Master breathed his last. His family was with him, together with many disciples, who for him were his spiritual family. The work which he left behind him is very great, achieved not only by the teaching which he gave, but also by the books he wrote, which have received recognition from the spiritual world, and marvellous reviews, in which the Master is often called a Wise Man and a Leader.

As much as he himself had prepared me for his death, the news of his departure from this life devastated me. Although in the last two months, because the state of his health was very bad, we didn't discuss my problems – I now did this with Mrs Klairi – I knew that he was there, that he was thinking of us and was sending us his positive thoughts and his love, and if a moment came when I felt the need to hear his voice, I could do so.

As soon as I was told what had happened, I shut myself in a room and for a long time was unable to react. At one point I felt two tears roll down my cheeks, but in spite of the fact that no one could see me, I hurriedly wiped them away, because at that moment I was carried away by the thought that, in order to show that I was acting correctly and dynamically, I had to stifle my emotions and not show them. I had forgotten how many times the Master had told me that we deal with problems with the mind and with love, that we can express the emotions providing that these are a manifestation of love and we can control them through the mind. On the contrary, I was attempting to suppress the emotion of sorrow which I felt, because I believed that in this way I would seem strong. Deep down, however, I was trying to hide another, stronger, emotion: my fear of death and the loss of the form, forgetting that these things are also parts of life.

I got up from my seat and left the room, thinking: "Very well, I won't cry, but there is no way that I'm going to attend the funeral". By taking this decision I felt somewhat better. Now I could think and seek the help of the inner Master. And he told me that my decision was a mistake, that I ought to accompany him on this journey to his last home and stop resisting what was a fact. The biological cycle of the Master's life had closed, as my own will close one day. I had, then, to stop fearing this end. What I had to fear was the stagnation of my spiritual development, which couldn't progress if I was not liberated from my fears and inhibitions.

On the day of the funeral, I stood alone in the back stall in the church and tried desperately to hold back my tears, without daring to approach the coffin. "You must draw yourself up to your full stature and not cry", I told myself continuously, "and don't operate through the emotions alone, through your solar plexus. But why not? Isn't this also a part of man? Aren't its manifestations those of life, of creation? If, as the Master used to say, we call it the 'solar spirit' and we think of it as such, then its manifestations will not only be attachment, desires, emotions, but will be love, freedom, thought, spirit."

I immediately removed my feet from where they were planted in the stall. With a firm step I went up to the coffin and stood a short distance from it. This time I let my tears flow freely. Perhaps some disciples didn't approve of such behaviour. But I continued to weep, because I felt that I was simply manifesting my love consciously, and not my fear of death or my sorrow alone.

At some point the sobs stopped. A calmness which I hadn't felt for a long time had taken their place; the emotions had become love, and my lips whispered: "Master, I feel the need to say a great 'thank you' to you for what you've done for me. You have taught me to believe that I am as weak as I am strong, as fearful as I am also fearless, as secure as I am insecure, but also how to work to unite all these pairs of opposite elements of myself, of life, so that balance will come. I cannot say that I always succeed, that sometimes I don't lose control of this balance, but now I'm not letting myself get lost in the emotions caused by my forms of resistance to some of these elements, because acceptance of them comes immediately, with my referral to their opposites, and so their unification and harmony are achieved.

It is certain, Master, that as long as I live, I shall feel profound gratitude for you. As an expression of that thankfulness, I have done what you proposed I should do: write a book. I know that it has its imperfections, that I haven't managed to give a rendering of all I have been taught in the depth that I was taught it, perhaps because I've not managed myself to reach that level. But I know, and this you taught me too, that what counts is the effort. And, honestly, Master, I've tried very hard."

EPILOGUE

About a year has passed since the day when I started my attempt to write this book, and this evening I've written its last page.

Sitting in an armchair, next to my husband's armchair, with my legs stretched out on a stool and my eyes closed, I am attempting to live again in my mind the 58 years of my life.

All those years unwind like a cinema film before my eyes. And whereas I see them roll by, and everything changing with their passage, something in this change remains the same. This is the image of myself. This image shows a frightened little girl who approaches everything with emotions. Her education doesn't help her when she is influenced by the emotions, and so her mind remains unused. The real meaning of love is unknown to her. Her step is unsteady, because every time she lifts her foot to go forward, she has the feeling that the ground will give way beneath the weight of her body. Under the influence of this fear, she hastily raises the other foot, for the next step. In this way, as the years pass, the footsteps become quicker, but her fears and insecurities grow greater.

In the end, in her efforts to stand upright, her life becomes an endless rush. Her anxiety makes her unable to see anything around her or to live really any moment of her life. Her only thought is herself, even if she believes that her life is full of service to others. She remains close to her loved ones and for many years she looks after them, but this is done, unconsciously, of course, out of obligation and fear of rejection by them, so that this help which she gives them brings about in her many conflicts of soul.

Her efforts to survive become greater, but her resistance to the negative aspects of people and of life generally also increases as the years go by. And so the moment comes when she realises, panic-stricken, that her powers have deserted her and that not only can she not run, she can't even walk. Panic and despair have taken the place of anxiety over her survival. And, while she believes that all is lost for her, that there is no salvation, that the rest of her life will be a torment and she will spend it curled up *on a sofa, trembling like an animal, God, judging perhaps that what she has been through out of ignorance may help her to find the path of truth, even now, guides her steps to the Master.*

He teaches her that all her fears and insecurities come from her great need for union with everybody and every-thing. This union, however, presupposes total acceptance of them, so that she can be brought through this to the ac-ceptance of her own self. Because her problem is due to the fact that she does not know the tragic truth – that she does not accept herself. The only path which will lead her to this is union with her partner, the other half of her self. Resistance to union, a consequence of fearing the restric-tion of her individual ego, is what has led her to imbalance of soul.

In the early days, her reactions against this truth are very strong. However, as her discipleship progresses, she begins to believe that things are exactly as she has been taught them. And she wonders: "How am I going to reveal all the things I don't accept in my partner, and, in any event, is it enough for me to work alone? And the other?". "What other?", the Master replies. "There is no other. He and you are one."

In the last year, the girl's picture has begun to change little by little, until its place has been taken by that of a mature woman, the one that I really am – a woman who has started to walk firmly on her legs. Through acceptance and love she has managed to change some things and has accepted that some others won't change. There are times when she goes off course, but she is brought back to it again by the words of the Master:

"The love of God is what created the world. And woman is a source of this love. By her love she can bring all things into balance, because woman is the soul of all things."

BIBLIOGRAPHY

Vasileiadis N.P.: *Orthodoxy and Feminism,* Athens: Brotherhood
of Theologists "THE SAVIOUR" 1992.

Delikostopoulos A.: *Hellenic Thought and Christianic Intellect,*
Athens: Apostolic Diaconia 1993.

Dimopoulos G.: *Inhouse Church,* Athens: Brotherhood of
Theologists "THE SAVIOUR" 1993.

Holzner J.: *Paul, (translation: former Archbishop of Athens
Ieronimos),* Athens: Damascus 1994 (13th edition).

Kakalidis D.: *The Wisdom of the Narrative,*
Athens: Megas Seirios 1992.

Kakalidis D.: *The Wisdom of the Poem,*
Athens: Megas Seirios 1994.

Lykiardopoulou K.: *The Man's Role in Contemporary Society,*
Athens: Megas Seirios 1985.

Lykiardopoulou K.: *The Woman's Role in Contemporary Society,*
Athens: Megas Seirios 1985.

Lykiardopoulou K.: *The Couple's Role in Contemporary Society,*
Athens: Megas Seirios 1985.

Lykiardopoulou K.: *The Master, Vol.I,* Athens:
Megas Seirios 1990.

Lykiardopoulou K.: *The Master, Vol.II,* Athens:
Megas Seirios 1991.

Lykiardopoulou K.: *The Master, Vol.III,* Athens:
Megas Seirios 1992.

Lykiardopoulou K.: *The Knowledge of the Educator,* Athens:
Megas Seirios 1994.

Lykiardopoulou K.: *Spiritual Healing,* Athens:
Megas Seirios 1995 (2nd edition).

Lykiardopoulou K.: *The Master, Vol.IV,* Athens:
Megas Seirios 1996.

Madders J.: *Stress and Relaxation (translation: Elli Emke)*
Athens: Psychogios 1983.

Marks I.M.: *Triumph over Phobia, (translation: M. Gregoriadou –
D. Triantafyllopoulos),* Athens: Lithi 1991.

Matsouka N.A.: *History of Byzantine Philosophy,* Thessaloniki:
Vanias 1994.

Nestoros I.-Vallianatou N.: *Composite Psychotherapy,* Athens:
Ellinika Grammata 1988.

Papadopoulos S.: *The Life of a Great One,* Athens: Apostolic
Diaconia 1994 (3rd edition).

Plato: *Symposium,* Athens: Kollaros & Co 1994.

Plato: *Timaios – Kritias,* Athens: Kaktos 1993.

Pythagoras: *Golden Verses (translation: Em. Pantelakis)* Athens:
Papyros 1978.

Tsolaka M.: *Anxiety, Depression: Prevention, Cure*
Athens: Hygeia – Zoi 1992.

Tsolaka M.: *Natural Hygiene and Orthodoxy,* Athens:
Hygeia – Zoi 1994.

Cooper J.: *Menopause (translation: Elli Emke),* Athens:
Ellinika Grammata 1988.

REVIEWS

It is with pleasure that I inform you that I have received your profound and brilliant work entitled The Path from Fear to Fearlessness.

We have studied with concentrated dedication your educative pages, clear as crystal, penetrating by degrees and with care the unknown and mysterious world of the soul.

This is an unhurried narrative, true and literary in every way, with a unique clarity and aesthetic quality which captures the mind.

At the same time, the basic feature of the sturdy dynamism which is inherent in this exceptional personal essay gives us the orientation of the correct way of dealing with the various problems of life, through the moral, philosophical, and psycho-social experiences left behind by the late lamented Master, Poet, and Thinker Dimitris Kakalidis.

Constantinos E. Daningelis – Director, Tripoli Public Library

I greatly appreciate your calm and distilled thought. Your manner of writing is simple and spare, certainly an advantage and virtue for the written word, and particularly for the essay.

You rightly draw attention to the daily trials of man because, of course, life means problems, as you aptly note. I wish you well at all times, and that we shall be aware of your thinking.

Vassilis A. Kyrkos – National and Capodistrian University of Athens

This is a moving experience testimony which deserves to be read by all those – and there are so many – who are possessed by fear and who are seeking a life-raft. Congratulations! You have given us something from your soul – literally. Best wishes.

Costas Liapis – Writer

Dimitris Kakalidis. He was a humanitarian, an essayist, a poet, but he will be remembered as the exceptional but unseen socio-spiritual teacher of brotherly love. He gave us a life's work of distinction. Two years after his unexpected death, his dis-

218

ciples continue to compose noteworthy accounts on the subject of his inspired teaching.

The path from fear to fearlessness also includes chosen items from D.K.'s teaching, which Ioanna Dimakou differentiates and successfully applies in the prose – in diary form – of her book.

In greater detail, we have a strong narrative of methodical and scientific citation of data, without, however, the flow of the story being distorted or neutralised. The author sifts the dialectic of meditation with sensitivity towards the Master Dimitris Kakalidis.

Manolis Pratsikas – Imerisios Kiryx newspaper, Patra

I liked your book very much, it is a gripping work – full of light, faith, and striving to win the miracle of life. This titanic struggle to emerge from the darkness into the light is so terrible that many fall in the process. [...] A few of the more fortunate and bold reach the summit. You had the courage and magnanimity to reach Olympus and be welcomed by the gods. I do not know any other way of expressing to you my admiration for your Herculean achievement.

I do not know what further I can write to you about your work, which moves to the depths of the soul, to its roots.

Vangelis N. Tertipis – Writer

Such books, of catalytic analysis, particularly of the psychological states which are a scourge to all of us, are truly rare in the prosaic times in which we live, in which books have ended up as a consumer commodity, and not a handing on of knowledge and wisdom. I have not read anything else by you, and this first contact, which meditates upon ways of escape from the oppression of phobia, was thrilling for me.

Dimitrios C. Halatsas – Writer

This is a work well produced with great care and weighed in your spiritual balance. It earns full marks, because it is a work of quality... A work which teaches man – every man.

I did not have the good fortune to meet your wise 'MASTER' in person. But I was proud to communicate with him spiritually, through his inimitable writings. I shall always remember him. In this I have been helped by that Greek lady (Klairi Lykiardopoulou) of rare spirituality, who has hymned him with so much love... He deserved it.

I believe that your offering to the memory of your 'MASTER', the 'MASTER', I believe, of so many people, is thoroughly invaluable.

In conclusion, I would like to agree with you that "The love of God is what created the world. And woman is a source of this love. By her love she can bring all things into balance, because woman is the soul of all things."

It could be said that this service to your fellow human beings, with so many cares and problems of everyday life, is specially important.

Alekos G. Chrysomallis – Writer

Ioanna Dimakou

Ioanna Dimakou was born in Novorosiski in Russia in 1938 and came to Greece in 1939. She studied economics and commercial sciences in Athens.

She married in 1965 and had two children, and worked at the Ministry of Economic Affairs for many years.

In 1990, she began to have psychological problems that manifested themselves mainly in the form of phobias.

In 1994, while the state of her health continued to be unchanged, she first visited the Master Dimitris Kakalidis, the founder of the Servers' Society Spiritual Centre. From him she learned a new way to deal with life and her problems, through the philosophical view that everything is part of life.

Her aim in writing the book is to describe the path she followed in order to overcome her phobias, a path that she continued to follow to attain her spiritual development.

www.ingramcontent.com/pod-product-compliance
Lightning Source LLC
Chambersburg PA
CBHW062223270326

41930CB00009B/1842